The Diversity of Exploitation

Studies in Critical Social Sciences Book Series

Haymarket Books is proud to be working with Brill Academic Publishers (www.brill.nl) to republish the *Studies in Critical Social Sciences* book series in paperback editions. This peer-reviewed book series offers insights into our current reality by exploring the content and consequences of power relationships under capitalism, and by considering the spaces of opposition and resistance to these changes that have been defining our new age. Our full catalog of *SCSS* volumes can be viewed at https://www.haymarketbooks.org/series_collections/4-studies-in-critical-social-sciences.

Series Editor
David Fasenfest (York University, Canada)

Editorial Board
Eduardo Bonilla-Silva (Duke University)
Chris Chase-Dunn (University of California–Riverside)
William Carroll (University of Victoria)
Raewyn Connell (University of Sydney)
Kimberlé W. Crenshaw (University of California–LA and Columbia University)
Raju Das (York University, Canada)
Heidi Gottfried (Wayne State University)
Alfredo Saad-Filho (Queen's University Belfast)
Chizuko Ueno (University of Tokyo)
Sylvia Walby (Royal Holloway, University of London)

THE DIVERSITY OF EXPLOITATION

On the Critique of Dominant Antiracism

EDITED BY
ELEONORA ROLDÁN MENDÍVIL
BAFTA SARBO

TRANSLATED BY
DANIELE PUCCIO

Haymarket Books
Chicago, IL

First published in 2024 by Brill Academic Publishers, The Netherlands
© 2024 Koninklijke Brill NV, Leiden, The Netherlands

Published in paperback in 2025 by
Haymarket Books
P.O. Box 180165
Chicago, IL 60618
773-583-7884
www.haymarketbooks.org

ISBN: 979-8-88890-576-0

Distributed to the trade in the US through Consortium Book Sales and Distribution (www.cbsd.com) and internationally through Ingram Publisher Services International (www.ingramcontent.com).

This book was published with the generous support of Lannan Foundation, Wallace Action Fund, and the Marguerite Casey Foundation.

Special discounts are available for bulk purchases by organizations and institutions. Please call 773-583-7884 or email info@haymarketbooks.org for more information.

Cover design by Jamie Kerry and Ragina Johnson.

Printed in the United States.

Library of Congress Cataloging-in-Publication data is available.

Contents

Foreword VII
Foreword to the English Translation XIV
Acknowledgments XIX
Notes on Contributors XX

1 Why Marxism? 1
  Eleonora Roldán Mendívil and Bafta Sarbo

2 Racism and Social Relations of Production: A Materialist Concept of Racism 16
  Bafta Sarbo

3 Social Reproduction, Gender, and Racism 36
  Eleonora Roldán Mendívil and Hannah Vögele

4 Racism in the European Migration and Border Regime from the Perspective of a Materialist Theory of Domination 51
  Fabian Georgi

5 Intersectionality, Identity, and Marxism 66
  Eleonora Roldán Mendívil and Bafta Sarbo

6 Police and Racism in Germany: A Historical Genesis 80
  Lea Pilone

7 Beyond the Class Compromise: Racially Segmented Labor Markets in the Context of Intra-EU Migration 95
  Celia Bouali

8 The Right-Wing Project and the Crisis of Capitalism: A Materialist Analysis of the Rise of the Right in Germany 114
  Sebastian Friedrich

9 Class and Racism: Notes for an Updated Understanding of Marxism 132
  Eleonora Roldán Mendívil

Index 139

Foreword

What used to be social criticism has degenerated into moral criticism of the behavior of individuals. Margaret Thatcher's 1987 dictum appears to have become the unspoken socio-theoretical foundation well into leftist circles: "There is no such thing as society. There are individual men and women [...] and they must look after themselves first." This basic assumption, when applied to the left, suggests that all problems, including those related to ecology, gender relations, racism, and even class relations, can be solved if individuals would purify themselves and behave correctly. The discussion of structural racism or sexism remains hollow because the concept of society can no longer be designated. Of course, Thatcher's assertion intended to sweep off the table the nasty word used to describe the core of societal misery: capitalism. For if there is no society, there also can be no capitalism, no social structures that set boundaries to however well-intentioned individual behavior premised on an omnipotent and now global system of reified relations. Furthermore, these boundaries become more invisible to the extent that there is a lack of collective struggles that can shake the foundations of this society. The fact that Thatcher's TINA, "there is no alternative" could become the sense of life to an entire generation was due to the abrupt end of radical class struggles after 1979. Capitalism and its way of socializing humans through objective commodity and monetary relations thus became such a self-evident and immutable aspect of daily life that it was hardly possible to discuss what was historically specific about this society.

The absence of a critique of capitalism as such, not only of its unsavory manifestations, which also disturb bourgeois minds and are now the focus of left debates, has shifted the entire matrix in which we locate racism, sexism, environmental destruction and many other forms of oppression and everyday humiliations. All these manifestations of capitalist exploitation and domination are now labeled only as "discrimination," and thus criticized only to the limited extent that they violate the bourgeois ideal of the formal equality of commodity owners. The fundamental class relation, based on the separation of the majority of people from the means of production and the consequent "silent compulsion" to sell their labor power in one form or another, is hidden and de facto legitimized by this standard of critique. The forms of oppression conceived as "discrimination" no longer bear any relation to the everyday exploitation of living labor, without which there could be no such thing as capital, profit, interest, and so on. The various forms of oppression are presented as discrete entities, capable of being addressed independently. This approach fails to acknowledge the interconnectedness of these issues and the larger social context within which they operate. The current trend of discussing "intersectionality" does not address the disappearance of society from critique, but rather reinforces it. The emphasis on multiple forms of discrimination attempts to more consistently bring the bourgeois ideal of equality into play, rather than to criticize its contradictions and limitations.

This theoretical deficiency corresponds to the disappearance of capitalism from practice. Collective rebellious struggles from below have been replaced by the state and the lone individual. What can or should the state do to give capitalism its "human face?" And how are the isolated, atomized individuals supposed to contribute to the humanity of society, that is of capitalism, by behaving and speaking as morally correct as possible (because there is not much more than speaking left to us in view of the absence of collective struggles)? Consequently, there is no longer a subjectivity that can offer an opposition and alternative to capitalist socialization in practice. This, in turn, restricts the intellectual scope of critique.

The texts in this edited volume were written by people who were born into an era in which capitalism appeared to be the only viable economic system and who are now questioning the connection between racism and the global capitalist system. The political discomfort with what the editors aptly call liberal anti-racism has recently been articulated more clearly. In a justifiably furious polemic, "the narcissism of the privileged" was recently dismantled and anti-racism staged as moral self-optimization was exposed (Berena, 2021). In a similarly eloquent and biting manner, Emma Dabiri's book, *What White People Can Do Next,* which playfully alludes to the moral self-optimization literature, dismantles the shortcomings of a liberal anti-racism which refuses to address capitalism (Dabiri, 2021).

The objective of this edited volume is to reintroduce the material and social, i.e. capitalist, roots of racism into the discussion and to relate serious anti-racism to the material struggles in this class society. The reasons why this important concern faces such significant challenges and why the texts are likely to generate heated discussions can be attributed to the history of the disassociation of anti-racism and class struggle. The struggles against racism or the oppression of women, which today are considered "identity politics," are contrasted with so-called class politics or are in fact referred to as "secondary contradictions" by the representatives of class politics, without explicitly using the term that is frowned upon. The concept originated in the social democratic women's movement of the 19th century, which had to subordinate the special needs and demands of women to the lofty goals and organizational unity of a party that claimed to represent the entire working class. The association of party or trade union politics with class struggle is a crucial basis for the contemporary juxtaposition of "identity" and "class." Both sides present a narrative of disintegration, albeit with reverse signs.

One perspective holds that a unified working class once engaged in a heroic struggle against capitalism. However, in the 1970s, the emergence of numerous "identities," including women, Blacks, gays, and lesbians, with their distinct interests, led to the dissolution of the once-harmonious proletariat, weakened the class struggle, and facilitated the triumph of neoliberalism. From the perspective of those who advocate for the interests of women, Black people, and migrants, it can be argued that these groups have consistently been marginalized within the context of the class struggle, as is evidenced by the historical record of social democratic party and trade union policy. The political consequences resulting from this picture are evident: those espousing a class position yearn for a return to the golden age of a social-democratically unified working class, while those representing "identity politics" are disillusioned and thus unable to recognize that the market economy is, in fact, a class society. The market and competition then appear to be more conducive to asserting one's own interests. This juxtaposition and the narrative on which it is based can be criticized theoretically, as the contributions in this volume seek to do. However, in practice it is not so straightforward to resolve as long as class politics remains as it is today and an alternative to market mechanisms seems impossible.

In her book *Family Values*, Melinda Cooper has identified the fundamental flaw in the entire narrative surrounding the struggles against a patriarchal gender system:

What challenged neoliberal criticism

> was not the New Deal welfare state itself (although neoliberals certainly had a long tradition of critique on this front) but rather the panoply of liberation movements that emerged out of and in excess of the postwar Keynesian order toward the end of the 1960s. At various moments between the 1960s and 1980s, poverty activists, welfare militants, feminists, AIDS activists, and public- interest lawyers articulated a novel politics of redistribution that delinked risk protection from the sexual division of labor and social insurance from sexual normativity. These movements were historically unique in that they continued to fight for greater wealth and income redistribution while refusing the normative constraints of the Fordist family wage.
>
> COOPER, 2017: 21

Similarly, A. Sivanandan had pointed out in an analysis of the "flight from class in the black movement" that the struggles of Black people in England were not a weakening but an enrichment of the class struggle, making it more global and explosive:

> So that when the trade unions refused to take up the cause of the Afro-Caribbean or Asian workers over industrial disputes or racial discrimination and/or exploitation, black communities closed ranks behind them and gave them the sustenance and the support to mount a protest or conduct a strike. And that then wove the interests of the class into the concerns of the community and made for a formidable political force far in excess of its numbers.
>
> SIVANANDAN, 1985: 2

These two assessments demonstrate that it was not the class struggle that was weakened by the explosive claims of various groups, but rather the containment and pacification of the class struggle that the welfare state and the integration of trade unions into it were intended to achieve after the war. What the women's and black movements criticized in the 1960s and 1970s was not the class struggle against capitalism, but the fact that the class struggle in its trade union form had resigned itself to capitalism in far too many ways instead of shaking the foundations of its rule. These foundations essentially include the hierarchies and divisions within the class that enable the maintenance of a stable order of exploitation in the first place.

Marx's critique of the fetish character of capital implies that it is only logical to understand the class struggle in its antagonistic dimension as a struggle of the class against itself. Capital is not an independent and overpowering subject in society, rather it is the reification of a social relationship, namely the fundamental relations of class and production. It is based on the daily labor of billions of proletarians, who are confronted with the product of their own labor as an alien subject by which they are subjugated. As Marx analyzes in Section IV of the first volume of *Capital* on the production of relative surplus value, this daily work and thus daily exploitation can only succeed if the class of those without property is divided in many ways and hierarchically structured by a "peculiar composition." The tumultuous struggles of the 1960s and 1970s posed a challenge to these hierarchies and prompted a re-evaluation of the power of capital in a more profound manner.

The explosive nature of the various rebellions forced the strategists of capital to react in an extremely repressive yet innovative manner. The year 1979/80 marked this turning point, signifying the abrupt end of struggles that still sought to overcome capitalism as such with a revolutionary claim. The drastic increase in interest rates in the US in 1979, the so-called Volcker Shock, redirected global capital flows and ended all fantasies of catch-up "development" in the Global South (Barker, 2019). Instead, military dictatorships came to power in Turkey and South Korea in 1980, which had already become the most important lever for containing the revolt in Latin America. The tragic transformation of the 1979 revolution in Iran, on which so many hopes had been placed in West Germany in particular, into a religious dictatorship contributed greatly to the abandonment of the idea of revolution altogether. Due to the dramatic defeat of the proxy war with the state in the so-called armed struggle, a revolutionary critique of capitalism had already fallen into disrepute. The left-wing projects were now called Eurocommunism and, in West Germany, above all it was the building of a Green Party, which increasingly ignored capitalism and class society.

In the autonomous scene, which emerged from the housing struggle at the beginning of the 1980s, an anti-capitalist language was still cultivated, but it was no longer possible to link this verbal criticism to the specific struggles. With regard to the momentum of anti-racist mobilizations, this was clearly demonstrated by the reactions to the so-called flood campaign of 1986. After the Chernobyl reactor disaster in April 1986 had plunged the legitimacy of state action into a deep crisis in the Federal Republic of Germany, the then Minister of the Interior Friedrich Zimmermann and others advanced the specter of an impending "flood of asylum seekers" in the summer and advocated for legal restrictions on the right of asylum. This led to the formation of "refugee groups" in many cities, which attempted practical solidarity work with refugees and protested against camp accommodation or deportations. However, it became virtually impossible to discuss how this could be combined with a critique of global capitalism. One final attempt to at least theoretically establish this connection and provide the refugee groups that emerged at the time with a political orientation was the so-called Medico paper from the same year, which originated from the *Autonomie/Neue Folge* magazine:

> How, then, is anti-imperialism to be conceived if not as a worldwide struggle on all fronts, as a struggle that simultaneously rebels against the rule of imperialism on all these fronts? And who should be the hegemonic social subject in this struggle, if not the majority of the world's population from the slums and camps? The simultaneity of Soweto and Toxteth, the land occupations in Mato Grosso and on Negros, the revolts in Cairo and Seoul, these are the points at which the anti-imperialist struggle is developing. It is challenging to determine the extent to which

social-revolutionary anti-imperialism can be spread, given the current situation of refugees. However, it is evident that the mobility of the world proletariat plays a crucial role in this process. The key question is how this mobility can be utilized in a self-determined manner and in ways that align with the interests of the proletariat. Should we assume a radical restructuring of the global population, the question remains as to whether this process will result in the productive reorganization of imperialism or an anti-imperialist struggle on a new level. Regardless of whether refugees ultimately reside in the camps or engage in illicit labor, they assert a claim to survival and compensation, and they are integral to the international class struggle.

To relate to them from an anti-imperialist position necessitates the defense of not only their right to asylum, but also their claim to freedom of movement, self-determination, and income. This entails the integration of the international class struggle into the metropoles and the protection of refugees from exploitation as a maneuvering mass of repressive social policy.

N.A., 1987

However, the theory and practice of anti-racism in the left scene also increasingly developed in the direction of liberal anti-racism, which was certainly also accepted as the lesser evil or the last possible resort under the impact of the new extreme right-wing and violent racism in Germany after 1989. In this sense, one of the first imports of newer theories from the US that addressed the local autonomous scene – the book *Three Into One: The Triple Oppression of Racism, Sexism and Class* by Klaus Viehmann et al.[1] which triggered a number of discussions in 1990 – also had an effect. It introduced the concept of triple oppression at a time when there was not yet any talk of intersectionality. Even then, it detached the question of anti-racism and anti-sexism from its connection with capitalism and offered the scene only the perspective of moral self-assurance. One critique at the time stated:

> The text reinforces the tendency of the autonomous left to get caught up in micro-contradictions, to detach itself from any social reality and ultimately only to engage with the outside world based on the certainty that 'we have the better morals.' This is then legitimized by 'they are sexist, they are racist, they are.' And this is precisely why the 'autonomists,' who

---

1 Free access in German: nadir.org/nadir/initiativ/id-verlag/BuchTexte/DreiZuEins/DreiZuEinsViehmann.html.

are constantly criticized in the text, tend to be confirmed in their attitude by reading it. Because in an increasingly chaotic world, it gives the certainty of being on the right side. But it gives little in the way of examining, understanding and politically intervening in the lively contradictions.

N.A., 1991[2]

With this brief and most incomplete review of the gradual disappearance of capitalism from left or radical left anti-racism, I only want to emphasize the importance of an edited volume like this in order to be able to once again develop a socio-critical perspective from below in the context of future debates and in political practice. Racism is not an accidental side effect of capitalism, rather it is structurally linked to it. A society that is systematically based on exploitation will always be dependent on forms of division and the degradation of people. These forms can change. Some may gain while others lose. However, this is the extent of the liberal anti-racism's contribution, since it refuses to question neither in theory nor in practice the class society of capitalism, which is disguised as a free market economy.

Christian Frings

Bibliography

Barker, Tim (2019) Other People's Blood, *n+1*, vol. 34, nplusonemag.com/issue-34/reviews/other-peoples-blood-2/.

Berena, 2021. Der Narzissmus der Privilegierten, *Young Migrants Blog*. youngmigrants.blog/2021/02/der-narzissmus-der-privilegierten.

Cooper, Melinda (2017) *Family Values: Between Neoliberalism and the New Social Conservatism*. New York: Zone Books.

Dabiri, Emma (2021) *What White People Can Do Next: From Allyship to Coalition*. New York: Harper Perennial.

N.A., 1991. Drei zu eins für wen? *Wildcat*, no. 57, pp. 38–40, wildcat-www.de/wildcat/57/w57_3zu1.htm.

N.A., 1987. Thesen zur Flüchtlingsfrage, *Wildcat*, no. 41, pp. 65–72, wildcat-www.de/wildcat/41/w41medic.htm.

Sivanandan, A. (1985) RAT and the degradation of black struggle, *Race & Class*, vol. 26, no. 4, 1985.

---

2 German source: wildcat-www.de/wildcat/57/w57_3zu1.htm; Response by Klaus Viehmann: wildcat-www.de/wildcat/58/w58_3zu1_replik.html.

Foreword to the English Translation

When we set out to write this anthology, our aim was to tie together different critical threads on identity politics we had been discussing with several leftist activists in Germany for some years. The intensification of identity-based social discourse, as well as the pandering of socialist organizations to identity politics, led us to believe that a Marxist intervention into this dynamic was necessary. Since Marxism and racism studies are very marginal within German-speaking academia, we set out to compile an anthology for this specific audience. Our hope was to write out some of our critiques to provide a basis for further discussions with our peers and comrades on questions of class and *race* in Germany. We never expected this book to interest anyone beyond the limited circle of committed comrades on the ground. Having published the first edition in September 2022 and presented it in a few German cities in October and November of the same year, we were amazed to see the overwhelming public interest in our book. Since we, Bafta and Eleonora, first published the book, we have travelled to more than 35 German, Austrian, and Swiss cities to read from this anthology to local audiences. After numerous book readings, public talks, key notes, and interviews, with the book now in its fourth edition, we realized the importance of a Marxist intervention specifically focused on the historical genesis of racism in Germany, on German identity politics. Marxism is not dead after all. On the contrary, young and old audience members alike were intrigued by our class analysis of racism.

Reflecting on the book's success, we also ask ourselves whether the book received such positive reviews due to what we do not talk about in it. Reviewers from very different and even opposing ends of the antiracist spectrum reached largely positive verdicts. We do not give a thorough analysis of the state or of German imperialism. Two topics that have a high potential for controversy – especially in Germany, with a left divided into often vulgar pro-imperialist and similarly vulgar anti-imperialist camps (the *Anti-Deutsche* vs. *Anti-Imp* divide). We also call for socialist organizing but what that exactly looks like and how or if political strategies can be concluded from this anthology is left open. Finally, even though we argue against identity-based politics and standpoint theory, the fact that we, Eleonora and Bafta, are non-white women in Germany makes a significant difference to many readers. In some cases, this very fact gave audiences the comfort to engage in critiques of identity politics without being suspicious it could be motivated by a hidden racist agenda. However, the fear that identity politics has become a right-wing slogan meant to discredit anti-racism and feminism in contrast to an imagined working class is not unwarranted.

This is unfortunate, we would like to add, because it shows the very retrograde state of anti-racism in Germany.

In Germany, the semantics of many political organizations, academic circles and activist/community spaces are permeated by analytical concepts and political slogans or programs emanating from the US in particular. While the literature and history of political organization from the anglophone world have undoubtedly enriched radical theory and practice, the unfortunate flip side of its dominance has been a retreat from analyzing the particular relations and history of German capitalism. Concepts such as whiteness and blackness that emerged during the early stages of US settler colonialism and slavery, and have since shaped racial discourse in the US, are uncritically adopted into a German context. Concepts such as BIPoC, meant to describe and differentiate the variety of negatively racialized groups in the US, are used in the German context, instead of developing its own particular analysis of racialization in Germany. Moreover, concepts developed in the academy and popularized on social media increasingly find their ways into political and activist spaces. Recently, more liberal examples include various forms of academic post-colonialism and decolonial theory production, more preoccupied with the epistemic, than with the material. Also, popular anti-racism literature on German bestseller lists have created a shift toward paradigms such as racial capitalism and decoloniality, which often sound radical but tend to exclude any form of class analysis or analysis of class struggle. In Daniele's view, the most important contribution made by Eleonora, Bafta, and the contributors to this anthology, is not merely their strong case for a return to Marxism, in particular with regard to the questions raised in this volume. It is their analytical rigor in demonstrating the current debates and providing answers with the help of a dialectical analysis and a thorough implementation of historical materialism. This shows the reader the rich and diverse traditions of Marxism concerning *race* and racism.

At the time of writing, the dynamics this book describes have intensified. While the German government is still committed to a liberal anti-racist rhetoric that embraces migration as long as immigrants are qualified for branches where the German labour market has shortages, deportations in Germany have already increased by 30–40 percent compared to the previous year (Santos, 2024). Right wing parties are the most popular political forces and racist incidences and violence on the streets have increased (Human Rights Watch, 2024). Anti-migrant sentiments are currently the main canalisation for discontent with German politics. Meanwhile the parliamentary and non-parliamentary left continues a moralizing discourse instead of understanding one's own actions of the past years as part and parcel of creating this problem.

Developments in Germany since the publication of this anthology can hardly be explained without the various enunciations of state-sanctioned, dominant anti-racism and approaches of intersectionality. While the last German Federal Election was supposed to signal the defeat of the preceding shift to the right, the unpopularity of the current liberal coalition government of the German Social Democrats, the Green Party and the Free Democratic Party, has in fact facilitated the rightward trend. In recent European elections, the ruling parties have suffered major defeats, while the conservative Christian-Democrats and far-right Alternative for Germany are now the most popular political forces. In the wake of the 2020 worldwide protest movement after the killing of George Floyd and growing anti-racist organizing in Germany after the racist murders in Hanau in February 2020, the Federal Elections of 2021 were shaped by those events. The government parties organized their political campaigns around questions of anti-racism, aspects of intersectionality, and climate change. While a faction of The Left Party, spearheaded by Sahra Wagenknecht, eventually split from the party for its alleged retreat from working class and anti-war politics in favor of identity-based issues, both the Social Democrats and the Green Party were able to form a government and fill important political positions with one of the most diverse Member of Parliament seating in Germany's history (Hänel, 2021). Suddenly, the post-Merkel era government was marked by an intersectional and feminist chancellor, Olaf Scholz. During his tenure as Senator for the Interior of Hamburg, he approved the forcible use of emetics, which killed several black men and was declared a form of torture by The European Court of Human Rights (Jackson, 2021). Further, foreign minister Annalena Baerbock introduced a feminist foreign policy agenda, and the Ministry of the Interior became headed by Nancy Faeser, who constantly stresses in words the importance of diversity and anti-racism to German democracy.

The contradictions emanating from such a rhetoric and the actual policies of the German states have taken new forms. During the 2022 World Cup in Qatar, Faeser wore a banned one-love band to take a stand for "diversity, women's rights and the rights of homosexuals (Der Spiegel, 2022)." Yet she saw no racism when confronted with the video of a Berlin police officer shouting "This is my country, you are a guest," as he was violently arresting an immigrant man inside his own home (TAZ, 2022). Moreover, the current liberal government has vastly increased its military budget, inaugurated the remilitarization of Germany and tightened its immigration laws (Boutelet, 2023; Deutsche Welle, 2024; Siebold, 2023). The ostensibly most liberal government of this decade has introduced unprecedented bans on constitutional rights, such as freedom of speech and freedom of assembly. In 2017, the Berlin Senate allowed a thousand neo-Nazis to march in commemoration of Hitler's deputy Rudolf Hess. The calls by some members of the public to ban it were dismissed on grounds that after careful examination it was found that "the liberal basic democratic order unfortunately also applies to assholes (WirtschaftsWoche, 2017)." By contrast, in 2022, all commemorations of the Palestinian Nakba were banned and followed by categorical bans of demonstrations related to Palestine, even weeks into the bombing of Gaza in October 2023 (Amnesty International, 2023). Then, chancellor Scholz appeared on the cover of *Der Spiegel* (2023), headlined "We must finally deport on a mass scale," and more recently Baerbock's feminist foreign policy has been forced to defend itself at the International Court of Justice against charges of aiding and abetting the Israeli genocide in Gaza (Van den Berg, 2024).

The events in Germany have particular characteristics. But they also reflect a larger trend evident in most capitalist states. The examples given above should remind us that both liberals and reactionaries employ these culturalist forms of identity politics, of anti-racism, of feminism etc. and therefore abstract particular social relations from the political economy that produces and sustains them. Consequently, if both the interpretation of and solution to a problem are located outside of the relations that produce and sustain it, the continued focus on the problem still serves to legitimate and reproduce the relations that create it. The Marxist tradition remains the most powerful tool to interpret and change the current dynamics.

Every place has its own history of racism – there are links and parallels, alongside differing developments that we need to study in their own right. Only through an engagement with the genesis of the particular forms of racism in Germany, can we – as people who live here and are committed to the struggle for socialism – become conscious of what these social phenomena actually represent. Hopefully, this will help us find forms to organize not only against racism but, by fundamentally questioning the capitalist mode of production, also for the universal freedom of humanity. Although we wrote this anthology with a German-speaking audience in mind, we believe that it can serve as an introduction into contemporary German society in general, and anti-racist politics in Germany in particular. By showcasing the particularity of racism in Germany, we offer an insight into how liberal politics travels continents and depoliticizes leftist radicals and socialists along the way.

Elenora Roldán Mendívil, Daniele Puccio and Bafta Sarbo
Berlin June 2024

Bibliography

Amnesty International. 2023. Germany: Protect the Protest: Against blanket bans of demonstrations for the rights of Palestinians, *Amnesty International*, Sep. 12, amnesty.org/en/documents/eur23/7180/2023/en/.

Boutelet, Cécile (2023) Germany takes tougher line on immigration, *Le Monde*, Nov. 7, lemonde.fr/en/international/article/2023/11/07/germany-takes-tougher-line-on-immigration_6234384_4.html.

Der Spiegel. 2022. Faesers "One Love"-Binde soll ins Haus der Geschichte, Nov. 24, *Der Spiegel*, spiegel.de/politik/deutschland/nancy-faeser-one-love-binde-soll-ins-haus-der-geschichte-a-e036b0f6-dba1-4810-980a-b6c690f02aa3.

Der Spiegel. 2023. Wir müssen endlich im großen Stil abschieben, Oct. 20, spiegel.de/politik/deutschland/olaf-scholz-ueber-migration-es-kommen-zu-viele-a-2d86d2ac-e55a-4b8f-9766-c7060c2dc38a?sara_ref=re-xx-cp-sh.

Deutsche Welle. 2024. Germany to hit NATO budget goal for 1st time since Cold War, Feb. 14, *DW.com*, dw.com/en/germany-to-hit-nato-budget-goal-for-1st-time-since-cold-war/a-68254361.

Hänel, Lisa (2021) The most diverse Bundestag yet gets ready to work, *DW.com*, Sep. 30, dw.com/p/414sU.

Human Rights Watch (2024) Germany, Events of 2023. World Report, *Human Rights Watch*, 2024, hrw.org/world-report/2024/country-chapters/Germany.

Jackson, James (2021) Olaf Scholz Is Not Your Friend, *Jacobin*, Sep. 26, jacobin.com/2021/09/olaf-scholz-german-election-merkel-credentials-scandals-chancellor-spd-coalition-machine-politics.

Santos, Ana P. (2024) Germany: Deportations up by 30% *InfoMigrants*, infomigrants.net/en/post/57652/germany-deportations-up-by-30.

Siebold, Sabine (2023) Germany pledges to make its military 'the backbone of defence in Europe,' *Reuters*, Nov. 9, reuters.com/world/europe/germany-pledges-make-its-military-the-backbone-defence-europe-2023-11-09/.

TAZ. 2022. Faeser sieht keinen Rassismus, *TAZ*, Sep. 22, taz.de/Uebergriff-der-Berliner-Polizei/!5883259/.

Van den Berg, Stephanie (2024) Germany denies accusation of aiding a genocide in Gaza at World Court, *Reuters*, Apr. 9, reuters.com/world/germany-denies-complicity-gaza-genocide-un-court-2024-04-09/.

WirtschaftsWoche. 2017 Grundordnung gilt leider auch für Arschlöcher, *wiwo.de*, Aug. 19, wiwo.de/politik/deutschland/innensenator-zu-neonazi-aufmarsch-grundordnung-gilt-leider-auch-fuer-arschloecher/20211262.html.

Acknowledgments

We want to thank David Fasenfest and Katie Short from Brill, for guiding us through the process of translation and believing that our German-language anthology had something to offer to an international audience. We would also like to thank the Rosa Luxemburg Foundation, who generously funded the translation. Further, we would like to thank Fiona Saya Roldán Clausen for helping with the final editing of the English translation.

The editors and the translator

Notes on Contributors

Celia Bouali
is a social scientist whose research focuses on the dynamics between class relations and migration. She has analyzed specific forms of exploitation that (EU-)migrant workers face in Germany. She has also worked on migrant labour struggles and organizing in German trade unions.

Sebastian Friedrich
is a journalist and author from Hamburg. In 2019, Berlin-based Bertz + Fischer published his book *Die AfD. Analysen, Hintergründe, Kontroversen* in a third and revised edition.

Christian Frings
is an activist, author and translator. Since the 1970s, he has been dealing with the critique of political economy of Karl Marx and the historical trajectory of global class struggles. For several years, he worked in metal factories in his home town of Cologne and took part in workers' struggles, squats, anti-racist struggles and other social movements. He has translated books and texts by Beverly Silver, Giovanni Arrighi, David Harvey, Vivek Chibber, Søren Mau and Walter Rodney. In the journal Prokla, he wrote about the significance of slavery in Marx's critique of economics. He regularly moderates reading groups on all three volumes of "Capital" and gives lectures on the history and theory of early operaism in Italy.

Fabian Georgi
PhD, is political scientist, educator and NGO worker at the Komitee für Grundrechte und Demokratie (Committee for Fundamental Rights and Democracy). From 2009 to 2013, he worked at the Philipps-University of Marburg, his last position being interim professor for political theory and the history of political ideas. He is Managing Director of the Assoziation für kritische Gesellschaftsforschung (AkG, Association for Critical Social Research) and a member of the editorial board of movements. Journal for Critical Migration and Border Regime studies. His research interests include political economy, political and social theory, especially state theory, migration and borders and social-ecological transformation. More information can be found at https://fabiangeorgi.de.

Eleonora Roldán Mendívil

is a political scientist and educator. She has worked in journalism, taught classes on intersectionality, racism, and colonial history at several universities in Germany and Austria. She is currently a PhD candidate at the University of Kassel's Department for Development and Postcolonial Studies in Germany. Eleonora has been a visiting scholar at the University of the Witwatersrand (2024/02–2024/04) in Johannesburg, South Africa, as well as at the Pontífica Universidad Católica del Perú in Lima, Peru (2024/05–2024/08). Her research interests include the Critique of Political Economy, (anti-)racism, gender relations, and the history of the development of global class struggle from the 18th through the 20th century.

Lea Pilone

is a history and law graduate from Freie Universität Berlin and is currently working as a research assistant in a law firm. She worked as a student assistant at the department for Criminal Law and Gender Studies at Freie Universität Berlin, where she taught classes on gender, class and race aspects within criminal law. As an author and speaker she focuses on Marxist legal critique, the contribution of criminal law to the reproduction of capitalism and a critique of the police abolition movement.

Bafta Sarbo

is a social scientist, educator and activist. She has taught and written on a Marxist analysis of racism, imperialism and police violence. She wrote a preface to the German reedition of Walter Rodneys How Europe Underdeveloped Africa. Bafta teaches courses on the three Volumes Marx' Capital at Rosa Luxemburg Foundation, has been active on the Board on the Initiative for Black People in Germany (2016–2024) and the broader antiracist movement in Germany focussing on police violence and refugee migration.

Hannah Vögele

is a political theorist, also trained in gender studies with interdisciplinary specialisations in history, law and social anthropology. Currently a Postgraduate Researcher at the Centre for Applied Philosophy, Politics and Ethics at the University of Brighton, UK, their research focuses on modern relations of property and propriety, (Germany's) colonial continuities, and feminisms' ambiguous histories. Hannah has an MPhil in Political Theory from the University of Oxford and has taught at different German universities in recent years. Amongst others, she is an editor of *Interfere: Journal for Critical Thought and Radical Politics*, is part of the theory collective SALT, and works on abolitionist thought and praxis in Berlin.

CHAPTER 1

Why Marxism?

Eleonora Roldán Mendívil and Bafta Sarbo

> The Marxist doctrine is omnipotent because it is true.
> VLADIMIR I. LENIN

∴

Marxism has been a marginalized discipline globally since the 1970s.[1] In Germany in particular, anti-communist policies such as the *Anti-Radical Decree* from 1972 onwards have driven Marxists out of universities and stigmatized them.[2] Marxism is now largely considered outdated, both in political discussions and in the universities. If Marxist theory is still employed at all today, it is typically in the form of liberal sociology, which replaces the foundations of Marxism with a canonization of Marx as an apolitical social theorist. In this context, the materialist method is typically rejected as reductive by accusing it of economism.

Karl Marx and Friedrich Engels formulated the materialist conception of history as a critical reaction to Hegel's ultimately idealist philosophy of history and Ludwig Feuerbach's scientific materialism. According to the materialist conception of history, people do not behave passively towards society, nor are they simply objects of history. Rather, human activity is the actual basis of all social processes. Dialectical materialism as a method claims to "understand everything that exists in the way it has become (Vellay, 2014: 35)" and thus always adopts a historical perspective: Social phenomena and their functioning can only be understood from the specific historical conditions of their emergence. This assumption also implies the changeability of social conditions. Only when these are historically contextualized and thus de-essentialized can the emancipation from relations of domination and violence become the

---

1 We would like to thank Daniele Puccio for helpful comments and criticism of this article.
2 The anti-radical decree was a resolution passed by the federal and state governments to check applicants for the civil service for their constitutional loyalty. See *Deutscher Bundestag* (2017). In practice, the anti-radical decree was primarily directed against socialists.

focus of analysis. Marx's critique of Feuerbach's anthropological materialism culminates in the well-known assertion that a mere view of society is insufficient: "Philosophers have only interpreted the world in various ways; the point, however, is to change it (Marx, 1987b: 5)." This is not only a political and ethical claim to theory, but also directly underlies the Marxist conception of history: "Men make their own history, but they do not make it just as they please; they do not make it under circumstances chosen by themselves, but under circumstances directly encountered, given and transmitted from the past (Marx, 1987a: 103)." This concept is central to Marxist theory, which posits that human activity, or labor, is the process by which people relate to their natural and social environment. This is opposed by liberal views of human societies. "Liberalism is the hegemonic ideology of bourgeois-capitalist society (Aquino et al, 2017)." For liberalism, the freedom of the individual is the highest category. In contrast to the liberal perspective, which regards the individual as the primary unit of analysis, a dialectical-materialist approach posits that society is not simply a sum of individuals. Rather, it is shaped by the manner in which people interact with each other to collectively organize the production and reproduction of their lives. As David Camfield notes:

> Marx 'relate[s] all aspects of the life process of society to economics.' But Marx's understanding of 'economics' is entirely different from how that term is generally understood today. It is emphatically not centred on technology or markets. Instead, the key concern is the social relations involved in processes of producing the means of human life.
>
> CAMFIELD, 2016: 293

A Marxist critique of capitalist societies thus encompasses not only the manner in which immediate production is organized, but also understands it in the totality of the social conditions under which it occurs. This includes the institutions and ideologies that contribute to its reproduction (Reed Jr, 2013: 49). Therefore, when Vladimir I. Lenin asserts that the strength of Marxism arises from the fact that it is "true," he specifically means that it is derived from reality. Marxism is therefore not isolated from real social movements, including those of the working class and other social movements such as anti-racist movements. It is therefore not a purely academic theoretical approach; rather it understands these movements as partial moments of the dialectic of capitalism and resistance, from which the categories on which our analysis is based are derived.

1   Allies Instead of Comrades

Our engagement with Marxist anti-racism began within anti-racist circles in Berlin. Based on practical considerations, we discerned the limitations of identity-based politics. In struggles for the right to stay or in the self-organization of People of Color or Black people, we engaged in a series of groups and alliances in which a politics of representation and the demand for diversity of the actors were central to radical left anti-racist everyday practice. We were thus part of a dynamic in which, for example, a person's social speaking position rather than the political content of their statements became the primary criterion for determining their radicalism.

In recent years, the concept of allyship has also become popular in this context. We would like to discuss this briefly, as it represents one of the cornerstones of retrograde politics in relation to anti-racism (Kiran and Vens, 2022). Allyship, describes being an ally. Those who are not negatively affected by any form of discrimination should form an alliance with those affected, informing themselves and educating themselves without demanding the support of those affected. The objective is to accumulate independent knowledge and assume responsibility for one's own actions. In contrast to the concept of comradeship, however, allyship is not defined by a common political stance and perspective, but by categories of social identity that, like the term itself, were largely imported from the US (Dean, 2019). Furthermore, alliance implies a temporary and expedient cooperation. A long-term common struggle with a common idea of society is rarely lived in political practice, even if it is verbally stated. This differs from a perspective that strives for general human liberation from a universalist standpoint. This perspective is not exclusively reserved for people with certain life experiences, but can be fought for as a common political orientation through programmatic exchange and collective practice. Without socialist antiracist alternatives in the Berlin left, we became increasingly frustrated with the dominance of liberal and identity politics approaches in anti-racist spaces. It became increasingly evident to us that the strategies for combating racism in Germany were often aligned with liberal approaches, despite the use of radical rhetoric. Initially, we undertook independent studies of socialist-antiracist forms of organizing in the United States and Marxist theorizing on racism in German and English-language literature. In 2017, we initiated a more collaborative approach, sharing ideas and jointly authoring a paper for the Rosa-Luxemburg Foundation's Marx200 conference in 2018 (Roldán Mendívil and Sarbo, 2021). Our attempt to revisit Marxist analyses of racism for the German context and make them relevant to the current anti-racism movement was met with a positive response, motivating us to compile materialist analyses of racism in the German-speaking world.

2 Radical Rhetoric and Liberal Praxis

In recent years, there has been a noticeable increase in the radicalization of anti-racist activism. There has been a growing demand for fundamental social change in activist and academic circles. In Germany, these demands have so far been expressed discursively through the selection of topics, campaigns and a more radical, even anti-capitalist rhetoric (Ayivi et al, 2021). However, it can also be observed that radical rhetoric is being appropriated by the bourgeois state, which employs it to disguise its structural logic, as well as by companies and non-governmental organizations, which utilize the aesthetics of these movements to enhance their marketability.[3]

This edited volume aims to provide anti-racists and leftists with the theoretical tools to transform the radicalizing political claim into an actual socialist policy. This requires a concrete analysis of the specific phenomena that need to be fought against.

3 Marx and Racism

In this context, however, we encounter several problems. In anti-racist spaces, the objection is raised that Marxism is a white men's ideology that cannot contribute anything to the analysis of the realities of non-white people's lives, partly because Marx himself did not write anything about the role of racism under capitalism. In this context, the accusation is often made that Marx himself argued in a racist manner. In particular, his use of racist terms in private letters[4] and his use of "Jew" and "Jewish" as synonyms for (financial) capital or capitalist in early writings such as "On the Jewish Question" from 1843 are cited as evidence of this (Marx and Engels, 1975b: 146–74). In order to address this criticism appropriately, we would like to briefly mention a few examples. It is evident that Marx engaged in personal hostility through the use of derogatory formulations directed towards physical features or character traits in

---

3 For a satirical discussion of this, see also: Browser Ballett (2020).
4 In a letter to Engels, for example, Marx referred to Ferdinand Lassalle, one of the founding fathers of German social democracy, as the "Jewish nigger Lassalle." See Marx and Engels, 1985b, 389.

numerous instances documented by Wulf D. Hund (Hund, 2018). However, we consider it a simplistic assumption to infer a particular racist attitude towards Blacks or Jews from private correspondence and the generalizations contained therein. Marx did, in fact, utilize common clichés about Black people or Jews in private letters and in some of his journalistic and academic writings. His polemics were repeatedly directed against Ferdinand Lassalle, who, as one of the fathers of reformist social democracy, was also a political opponent within the socialist movement. The vast majority of Marx's texts are full of mockery and irony. For example, his statements on the Germans as a naive people whose emancipation as human beings was still pending:

> As philosophy finds its material weapon in the proletariat, so the proletariat finds its spiritual weapon in philosophy. And once the lightning of thought has squarely struck this ingenuous soil of the people, the emancipation of the Germans into men will be accomplished.
> MARX, 1844

It is evident that the racist and derogatory nature of various designations and statements cannot be dismissed as mere mockery in a world in which racist arguments were used to justify violence, enslavement and structural mistreatment. However, we consider his political actions to be pivotal: Throughout his life, Marx campaigned for the political equality of Jews[5] and actively supported the struggle against slavery in the Americas. Marx wrote about abolitionism in the US as early as 1848/49 in the *Neue Rheinische Zeitung* (Heideman, 2018: 5). In 1860, Marx emphasized to Friedrich Engels that the slave movement in America was one of the most significant events of the time.[6] In a letter to the newly re-elected US President Abraham Lincoln in 1864, Marx placed the still raging civil war in the US in a global context and emphasized that the outcome of the war would help determine the future of the class struggle worldwide: "The working men of Europe feel sure that, as the American War of Independence initiated a new era of ascendancy for the middle class, so the

---

5 In 1843, without hesitation, he signed a petition for the equality of Jews. See Marx, 1975a, 400.
6 "In my view, the most momentous thing happening in the world today is the slave movement – on the one hand, in America [...] Thus, a 'social' movement has been started both in the West and in the East. Together with the impending *downbreak* in Central Europe, this promises great things." See Marx and Engels, 1985b: 4; August H. Nimtz even describes how Marx mobilized the German-American community in the US against slavery and even agitated against slavery among workers in Britain, which led to demonstrations by British workers against the British government's interference on behalf of the Confederacy (Nimtz, Jr, 2003: 118–21).

American Anti-Slavery War will do for the working classes (Marx and Engels, 1985a: 40)."[7]

Contrary to what Cedric J. Robinson asserts in *Black Marxism: The Making of the Black Radical Tradition*,[8] Marx was well aware of the economic significance of slavery for the specific capitalist mode of production:

> The discovery of gold and silver in America, the extirpation, enslavement and entombment in mines of the aboriginal population, the beginning of the conquest and looting of the East Indies, the turning of Africa into a warren for the commercial hunting of black-skins, signalised the rosy dawn of the era of capitalist production.
>
> MARX, 1996: 739

Marx addresses the role of racism within the working class in his discussion of the division of the English working class into English and Irish workers:

> All industrial and commercial centres in England now have a working class *divided* into two *hostile* camps, English proletarians and Irish proletarians. The ordinary English worker hates the Irish worker as a competitor who forces down the standard of life. In relation to the Irish worker, he feels himself to be a member of the *ruling nation* and, therefore, makes himself a tool of his aristocrats and capitalists *against Ireland*, thus strengthening their domination *over himself*. He harbours religious, social and national prejudices against him. His attitude towards him is roughly that of the *poor whites* to the niggers in the former slave states of the American Union. The Irishman pays him back with interest *in his own money*. He sees in the English worker both the accomplice and the stupid tool of *English rule in Ireland*.
>
> MARX, 1988: 474–75

---

7 However, Wulf D. Hund criticizes the fact that in this letter Marx describes the struggle for territories as the development of "virgin soil" through the "labour of the immigrant" and thus negates the existence of indigenous societies on these territories in a colonial-racist manner (Hund, 2018: 121).

8 "Marx consigned race, gender, culture, and history to the dustbin. Fully aware of the constant place women and children held in the workforce, Marx still deemed them so unimportant as a proportion of wage labor that he tossed them, with slave labor and peasants, into the imagined abyss signified by pre-capitalist, noncapitalist, and primitive accumulation (Robinson, 2020: XLIX)."

Although Marx did not develop a general theory of racism from this observation, we do find methodological tools here that can be used to analyze socially specific formations such as racism and class division.

A critique inspired by postcolonial theory engages with Marx's explanations of non-European modes of production. Here, for example, Marx's 1853 essay "The Future Results of British Rule in India," which features prominently in Edward Said's work *Orientalism*, published in 1978, is cited (Said, 1979: 153–57; Marx, 1979: 217–22). This early journalistic article by Karl Marx, who was living in exile in Britain, was published in the *New-York Daily Tribune*. Marx analyzed how British capital secured its colonial military and political power "through blood and dirt" in India (Marx, 1979: 221). Convinced of the necessity to industrialize India as a prerequisite for the possibility of liberation from British colonialism, Marx described the destructive and simultaneously regenerative mission of the British as follows: "England has to fulfill a double mission in India: one destructive, the other regenerating – the annihilation of old Asiatic society, and the laying the material foundations of Western society in Asia (Ibid: 217–18)." Marx had previously correctly described the specifically Indian social order as one of "paramount power" of the monarchical Moguls and Viceroys, as a society divided "between caste and caste. (Ibid: 217)" He added that India could not "escape the fate of being conquered" as "the whole of her past history [...] has been the history of the successive conquests she has undergone." He therefore stated that Indian society had "no known history (Ibid)." "What we call its history, is but the history of the successive intruders who founded their empires on the passive basis of that unresisting and unchanging society (Ibid)."

This static image of a society that is in reality far more complex in economic, social and political terms demonstrates Marx's "epistemic Eurocentrism (Achcar, 2013: 83)." Gilbert Achcar describes how Karl Marx and Friedrich Engels' examination of non-European societies was based entirely on European sources. Marx and Engels were thus "hostages to these limitations of their epoch, delving into the flawed European knowledge of non-European societies that was the only one available to them (Ibid)." Cedric Robinson advances a further claim, namely that,

> at its epistemological substratum, Marxism is a Western construction – a conceptualization of human affairs and historical development that is emergent from the historical experiences of European peoples mediated, in turn, through their civilization, their social orders, and their cultures.
> ROBINSON, 2020, 2

Achcar contrasts this epistemic Eurocentrism with an understanding of political internationalism by describing how the claim to emancipation in Marx's thinking was actually not Eurocentric, but valid universally. Moreover, Marx has repeatedly and radically changed and reconsidered his positions on colonialism, which Kevin B. Anderson elaborates in a detailed study of his late anti-colonial writings (Anderson, 2016). Furthermore, academic writings intended for publication cannot be equated with private letters. It is therefore necessary to contextualize these statements, as the language and tone of Marx and his environment cannot be measured in terms of our current understanding, with which we react much more sensitively to insults based on origin or appearance. It is neither surprising nor particularly special that Marx also used racist ascriptions in his everyday life. The decisive factor for us is the method of scientific socialism, which he significantly shaped, while the criticism of his verbal racist derailments is primarily a moral argument. This moralism projects anti-racist positions, which today are supposedly taken for granted, into a time when the struggles that made today's self-evident positions possible had not yet taken place. Of greater consequence than Karl Marx's personal positions as a historical figure is the dialectical-materialist method he developed and the tradition of Marxist theorizing. This tradition is embedded in numerous socialist movements across the globe, from China to the African continent to Latin America, in which Marxism has been further developed, and is therefore important for socialists today. The assertion that Marxism is a white man's ideology not only ignores the global intellectual history of Marxism. It would also have to explain why the universalism of human liberation should only be valid for Europeans and their descendants, but not for all other people. Instead, we understand Marxism as a valid and applicable theoretical framework that is not contingent on time or place. A Marxist analysis necessitates contextualization and formulates a universal claim for all human societies based on generalized economic laws of motion (Rodney, 1975).

4 Racial Capitalism?

One concept that is currently gaining popularity in the English-speaking world is racial capitalism. In 1983, Cedric J. Robinson published *Black Marxism: The Making of the Black Radical Tradition* in London, which used the concept as the basis for his critique (Robinson, 2020). Until the year 2000, this work had little influence on debates about *race* and capitalism in the English-speaking academic world. It was not until its reissue, which included a foreword, that racial capitalism emerged as a radical alternative to culturalist and liberal analyses of *race* and racism in the English-speaking humanities (Burden-Stelly, 2020). Not least since the new edition of 2020 including a foreword by Robin D. G. Kelley, the concept has regained popularity.

The term first emerged in the 1970s, as documented by Arun Kundnani (2020). At that time, the anti-apartheid movement advocated for an international boycott of South African exports. Opponents of the boycott contended that economic growth and continued industrialization would weaken racism in South Africa. Martin Legassick and David Hemson offered a contrasting perspective. In their 1976 text entitled "Foreign Investment and the Reproduction of Racial Capitalism in South Africa," they demonstrated "that South African racism was strengthened, not weakened, by capitalist growth. Capitalism was not the solution to racism, but the soil upon which it grew (Ibid)." Legassick and Hemson were part of a group of South African Marxists who began to use the term racial capitalism in the 1970s to analyze the political economy of apartheid South Africa. Harold Wolpe and Neville Alexander were also part of this group (Ibid). Alexander's critique of colonial apartheid South Africa emphasized the problems of economic domination and exploitation. His refusal to consider the idea of race in abstraction from the more fundamental historical development of capitalism has led to his academic and political isolation over the years (Cloete, 2014). Unlike the historically and geographically specific South African analysis of Alexander's group, Robinson takes up the concept to describe the development of capitalism universally:

> The development, organization, and expansion of capitalist society pursued essentially racial directions, so too did social ideology. As a material force, then, it could be expected that racialism would inevitably permeate the social structures emergent from capitalism.
> ROBINSON, 2020: 2

Robinson does not consider a radical break in the transition from feudalism to capitalism, but describes a "racializing" continuity based on the diverse forms of socio-linguistic-cultural distinction in pre-capitalist Europe (Ibid: 10–28). Racial capitalism as a concept thus builds on the "social, cultural, political, and ideological complexes of European feudalisms (Ibid: 10)."

> As an enduring principle of European social order, the effects of racialism were bound to appear in the social expression of every strata of every European society no matter the structures upon which they were formed.
> Ibid: 28

Currently, the term racial capitalism is hardly discussed in the German-speaking world and we will not be working with it in this edited volume.[9] However, since this concept is becoming increasingly prominent among Marxist scholars in the English-speaking world, we will briefly outline why we are not using it.

We are generally skeptical of categories that do not understand capitalism as a form of production and society in itself, but ascribe to it specific forms of super-exploitation, oppression and destruction as immanent and general characteristics. It is conceivable that capitalism could function without racism – other formations of the mediation of exploitation and super-exploitation could theoretically take its place. The fact that they exist today is contingent and historically determined. In relation to the more universal racial capitalism model defined by Robinson, we are not convinced that pre-capitalist socio-linguistic-cultural distinctions in Europe can be historically understood as a form of *race*. On the contrary, we recognize a clear break with the medieval and early modern lines of distinction based on regionalisms in the emergence of modern biologistic racial theories at the end of the 18th and beginning of the 19th century. For us this implies that, the racial in racial capitalism is not a historical constant in the development of first European and then global productive forces, but a specific form of rationalizing the mediation of capital and labor in the course of the 18th and 19th centuries in Europe and its colonies. The specific form of capitalist production and thus society that we find in Germany is shaped by racism. However, these racisms are themselves in constant motion and transformation, and in different historical periods, depending on crises and benefits, they also assume new roles, some of which are detached from the economic base.[10] However, the German national economy and the nation state that emerges from it and feeds back into it is not only structured by racisms. A number of forms of super-exploitation are based on capitalist gender and sexual relations. Consequently, it would be more accurate to refer to it as *racial gendered sexual capitalism* and we could add numerous other adjectives to describe what is already contained in the term capitalism.[11] Therefore, we believe that the term racial capitalism is based on premises that we reject, which is why we will not use it in this edited volume.

---

9 There are exceptions, such as Thompson (2022).
10 See the contribution by Bafta Sarbo in this volume, pp. 37–63.
11 An example of a continuous adjectivization would be bell hooks' term *imperialist white supremacist capitalist patriarchy*. See hooks, 2013: 4–5.

5   Marxism in Germany

The objective of this edited volume is to intervene in the Marxist debates in German-speaking countries, which tend to neglect addressing racism. While theoretical discussions on racism in German-speaking countries were sporadic during the 20th century, there has been little subsequent development.[12] In contrast, English-speaking countries have made significant strides in this area, with the debate and the movement against racism being much more advanced. While some of the findings from these debates can be applied to the German context, they are not a substitute for an examination of specific German conditions. In Germany, the lack of debate is expressed, among other things, by a kind of linguistic impotence. As a consequence of the anti-racist protests in 2020, it was decided in 2021 at the request of the Bündnis 90/Die Grünen parliamentary group in the Bundestag to remove the term *Rasse* from the German Basic Law.[13] In the social sciences, a similar position is held on the issue, with *race* being used instead of *Rasse*. It is argued that the English term is less ambiguous and less loaded, given the history of the term *Rasse* in German and its use under National Socialism (Messerschmidt, 2011). Furthermore, the term racial is said to have no genocidal connotations in English, whereas the German term *Rasse* is said to have such connotations (Khakpour et al.). However, the English-language usage is also burdened by British colonialism and the resulting settler colonies, including apartheid and racial laws, and it would have to be proven first that the term has a social rather than a biological connotation in English, as is claimed. In German-speaking academia, on the other hand, the term *Ethnie* (ethnicity) is commonly used today. This term should replace the term *race*, but it is also problematic: It trivializes the implications of this category and creates the impression that it is unproblematic and not constructed by racism. We therefore emphasize the use of the term *Rasse* because we believe that the history of this term cannot be linguistically eliminated by using the English term *race*, and rather that it is indispensable in order to be able to talk about racism as social mediation within societies.

---

12 Here we would like to refer to German-language attempts to develop a Marxist or at least partially materialist concept of racism: See Schmitt Egner, 1978: 350–405; Ruf, 1989: 63–84; Kalpaka et al, 2017; the Kanak Attak network and associated racism scholars such as Manuela Bojadžijev, Serhat Karakayalı, Mark Terkessides and Vassilis Tsianos.

13 The problematization of the term is significantly older than the protests, but it was these protests that created the social climate that made this vote possible with the corresponding result. Cf. Deutscher Bundestag, 2021.

The title of this volume, *The Diversity of Exploitation*, contains a double meaning. On the one hand, it refers to the different conditions of exploitation to which groups of workers are exposed, as discussed in some of the contributions. Consequently, despite there being an average level of exploitation in society that establishes the remuneration and working hours, legal distinctions between different population groups, for instance according to their residential status, present a potential to subvert this level.[14] It is in this context that we speak of super-exploitation. This also means that, due to the different conditions of exploitation, life situations and immediate interests within the working class are differentiated. We can therefore understand the divided working class as, among other things, a product of the different conditions of exploitation, the diversity of exploitation.

Secondly, the title addresses the popular buzzword of diversity. The recognition and highlighting of different identities are often presented today as a strategy against racism. However, this diversity refers above all to the new demands that capital places on its workforce, who are more in demand as subjects with their own individual characteristics.[15] The subtitle "On the critique of dominant anti-racism" points to the intention and direction of this edited volume. It is about a critique of the dominant liberal anti-racism, but also about alternatives to it. It can be easily integrated into the bourgeois state and reconciled with corporate interests because it does not question the foundations of capitalist class society. Indeed, it is often even argued from within its logic, where racism is primarily problematized as a disadvantage in locational competition and in the acquisition of labor.[16]

Within this thematic complex, the contributions in this edited volume deal with different aspects of the theory and praxis of anti-racism in Germany. Despite their different emphases, all the contributions are unified by a dialectical-historical-materialist approach to questions pertaining to the relationship between class and race.

All quotations from foreign-language texts were translated into English for this volume by the translator.

---

14   Examples of this are apartheid laws, but also general forms of legislation on foreigners.
15   See the second contribution by Eleonora Roldan Mendivil and Bafta Sarbo in this volume, pp. 66–79.
16   "Furthermore, Germany is acting in its own interest if it prevents the emigration of people with experience of racism. [...] Germany has spent thousands of euros on their education and they are excellent workers. [...] Germany cannot really afford their emigration in times of skills shortages (Schearer-Udeh, 2017)."

Acknowledgements

Finally, we would like to express our gratitude to all those who have contributed to this project over the months and years. We would like to begin by thanking the authors of the articles: Celia Bouali, Sebastian Friedrich, Fabian Georgi, Lea Pilone and Hannah Vögele. Despite the adverse circumstances presented by the pandemic, including postponements and commitments such as full-time employment or studies, childcare or thesis work, they provided insightful and original contributions. The discussions surrounding their contributions have enriched and sharpened our analyses. Our special thanks go to Debora Darabi, who provided content and editorial support for the contributions. Another special thank you goes to Sebastian Friedrich, who supported this project in the search for a publisher even before we asked him for his own contribution and who was available to advise us over a longer period of time. We would also like to thank Christian Frings in particular for his meticulous and generous proofreading and editorial comments, as well as for his guidance throughout the entire process, from the initial idea to the search for a publisher and the realization of this project. We would also like to thank Martin Beck and the entire team at Dietz Verlag for their openness and flexibility throughout the process and for their confidence in this volume.

Bibliography

Achcar, Gilbert (2013) *Marxism, Orientalism, Cosmopolitanism*. London: Saqi, 2013.

Anderson, Kevin B. (2016) *Marx at the Margins. On Nationalism, Ethnicity, and Non-Western Societies*. Chicago: University of Chicago Press.

Aquino, Amanda Trelles et al. (2017) Zur Lage des Antirassismus, *Lower Class Magazine*, June 27, lowerclassmag.com/2017/06/27/debatten beitrag-zur-lage-des-antirassismus.

Ayivi, Simone Dede et al. (2021) Rassismus in Deutschland nach George Floyd, *Rechtsaussen*, rechtsaussen.berlin/2021/09/rassismus-in-deutschland-nach-george-floyd.

Browser Ballett, 2020. Image-Pflege dank Rassismus, *YouTube video*, June 13, youtube.com/watch?v=yp9Z1B_3jmY.

Burden-Stelly, Charisse (2020) Modern U.S. Racial Capitalism. Some Theoretical Insights, *Monthly Review*, vol. 72, no. 3, pp. 8–20, monthlyreview.org/2020/07/01/modern-u-s-racial-capitalism.

Camfield, David (2016) Theoretical Foundations of an Anti-Racist Queer Feminist Historical Materialism, *Critical Sociology*, vol. 42, no. 2, pp. 289–306, DOI: 10.1177/0896920513507790.

Cloete, Michael (2014) Neville Alexander: Towards overcoming the legacy of racial capitalism in post-apartheid South Africa, *Transformation. Critical Perspective on Southern Africa*, vol. 86, pp. 30–47, DOI: 10.1353/trn.2014.0032.

Dean, Jodi (2019) *Comrade. An Essay on Political Belonging*. London: Verso.

Deutscher Bundestag (2017): Der sogenannte "Radikalenerlass" in der deutschen und europäischen Rechtssprechung, August 17, bundestag.de/resource/blob/526404/effe56fccef64bc4c32baaeb0c4ce495/wd-3-125- 17-pdf-data.pdf.

Deutscher Bundestag (2021): Experten mehrheitlich für Ersetzung des »Rasse«-Begriffs im Grundgesetz, June 21," bundestag.de/dokumente/textarchiv/2021/kw25-pa-recht-rasse-847538.

Heideman, Paul (2018) *Class Struggle and the Color Line*. Chicago: Haymarket Books.

hooks, bell (2013) *Writing Beyond Race: Living Theory and Practice*. New York and London: Routledge.

Hund, Wulf D. (2018) Der 'jüdische Nigger' Lassalle. Marginalie zu einem Brief von Karl Marx. *Sozial.Geschichte Online*, vol. 24, pp. 103–30, DOI: 10.17185/duepublico/47940.

Kalpaka, Annita et al. (2017) *Rassismus. Die Schwierigkeit, nicht rassistisch zu sein*. Hamburg: Argument Verlag.

Khakpour, Natascha et al. (2020) *Vorwort des Editorial Boards zur Begriffsarbeit bei der Übersetzung von Stuart Hall: Vertrauter Fremder. Ein Leben zwischen zwei Inseln*. Hamburg: Argument Verlag, argument.de/wp-content/uploads/2021/09/Begriffsarbeit-bei-der-deutschen-Ausgabe-von-Stuart-Hall.pdf.

Kiran, Cantürk and Hartwig Vens (2022) Das Unbehagen am Konzept "Allyship," *Deutschlandfunk Kultur*, February 13, deutschlandfunkkultur.de/kritik-konzept- allyship-100.html.

Kundnani, Arun (2020) What is racial capitalism? Talk at Havens Wright Center for Social Justice, University of Wisconsin-Madison, October 23, kundnani.org/what-is-racial-capitalism.

Marx, Karl (1975a) To Arnold Ruge. March 13. In Karl Marx and Frederick Engels, *Collected Works Vol. 1*. London: Lawrence and Wishart.

Marx, Karl and Frederick Engels (1975b) On the Jewish Question. In *Collected Works Vol. 3*. London: Lawrence and Wishart.

Marx, Karl and Frederick Engels (1985a) Karl Marx to Abraham Lincoln, President of the United States of America. In Karl Marx and Frederick Engels, *Collected Works Vol. 20*. London: Lawrence and Wishart.

Marx, Karl and Frederick Engels (1985b), *Collected Works Vol. 41*. London: Lawrence and Wishart.

Marx, Karl (1979) The Future Results of British Rule in India. In *Collected Works Vol. 12*. London: Lawrence and Wishart.

Marx, Karl (1988) Marx to Sigfrid Meyer and August Vogt. April 9, 1870. In Karl Marx and Frederick Engels, *Collected Works Vol. 43*. London: Lawrence and Wishart.

Marx, Karl (1996) Capital: A Critique of Political Economy, Volume 1. In Karl Marx and Frederick Engels, *Collected Works Vol. 35*. London: Lawrence and Wishart, 1996.

Marx, Karl (1844) Introduction to A Contribution to the Critique of Hegel's Philosophy of Right. In *German-French Annals*, February 7 and 10, marxists.org/archive/marx/works/1843/critique-hpr/intro.htm.

Marx, Karl (1987a) The 18th Brumaire of Louis Napoleon. In Karl Marx and Frederick Engels, *Collected Works Vol. 11* London: Lawrence and Wishart.

Marx, Karl (1987b) Theses on Feuerbach. In Karl Marx and Frederick Engels, *Collected Works Vol. 5*. London: Lawrence and Wishart.

Messerschmidt, Astrid (2011) Rassismusanalyse in der postnationalsozialistischen Gesellschaft. In Paul Mecheril and Claus Melter (eds.), *Die haben gedacht, wir waren das. Migranten über rechten Terror und Rassismus*. Köln: Papyrossa, pp. 59–74.

Nimtz, Jr, August H. (2003) *Marx, Tocqueville, and Race in America: the "Absolute Democracy" or "Defined Republic."* Lanham: Lexington Books.

Reed Jr, Adolph (2013) Marx, Race and Neoliberalism, *New Labor Forum*, vol. 22, no. 1, pp. 49–57, DOI: 10.1177/1095796012471637.

Robinson, Cedric J. (2020) *Black Marxism: The Making of the Black Radical Tradition*. Chapel Hill: UNC Press.

Rodney, Walter (1975) Marxism and African Liberation, *Marxists.org*, marxists.org/subject/africa/rodney-walter/works/marxismandafrica.htm.

Roldán, Mendívil, Eleonora and Bafta Sarbo (2021) Materialistischer Antirassismus – zurück zu den Wurzeln. In Judith Dellheim et al. (eds.): *Auf den Schultern von Karl Marx*. Münster: Westfälisches Dampfboot, 2021, pp. 297–309.

Ruf, Werner (1989) Rassismus und Ökonomie. In Otger Autara et al., *Theorien über Rassismus. Eine Tübinger Veranstaltungsreihe*. Hamburg: Argument Verlag, pp. 63–84.

Said, Edward (1979) *Orientalism*. New York: Vintage Books.

Schearer-Udeh, Jamie (2017) Vielfalt ist Widerstand, *Zeit Online*, October 4, zeit.de/gesellschaft/zeitgeschehen/2017-10/antirassismus-aktivistin-afd-rassismus-rechtspopulismus-jamie-schearer-udeh?utm.

Schmitt Egner, Peter (1978) Wertgesetz und Rassismus. Zur begrifflichen Genesis kolonialer und faschistischer Bewusstseinsformen, *Gesellschaft. Beiträge zur Marxschen Theorie*, vol. 8/9, pp. 350–405.

Thompson, Vanessa E. (2022) Von Black Lives Matter zu Abolitionismus, *analyse & kritik*, vol. 683, pp. 17–18.

Vellay, Claudius (2014) Dialektik und historischer Materialismus. In: Ingrid Artus et al, *Marx für SozialwissenschaftlerInnen. Eine Einführung*. Wiesbaden: Springer VS.

CHAPTER 2

Racism and Social Relations of Production: A Materialist Concept of Racism

Bafta Sarbo

> Slavery was not born of racism: rather, racism was the consequence of slavery.
> ERIC WILLIAMS

∴

The fact that racism has not been abolished following the refutation of the existence of biological races is evidenced today by racist police violence, right-wing attacks and murders as well as racialized socio-economic inequality both in Germany and globally. The unequal distribution of racialized people across the different classes alone indicates that there must be a connection between racism and class affiliation. Marxism has historically emphasized the connection between racism and class society and the slogan "racism divides the working class" has become a dictum. However, despite repeated assertions, there has been a lack of theoretical evidence to substantiate the connection between racism and capitalism, as Peter Schmitt-Egner observed in the 1970s (Schmitt-Egner, 1978).

Particularly in Germany, an ethnically segregated labor market is perceived as the result of racism or so-called xenophobia and is therefore primarily the subject of anti-discrimination policy. Regardless of whether racism is conceptualized as an ideological discourse or as internalized images of "the other," it is generally regarded as a concept that primarily reduces racism to issues of consciousness. This aligns with an anti-racism that aims to dismantle racism primarily in consciousness.

There is a widespread notion that the problem of *race* ideology can be attributed to a fallacy in the natural sciences, which incorrectly assumed the existence of human races. This fallacy, and therefore racism, can be resolved or has already been resolved by correcting this scientific error. Such idealism, which assumes that society is as it is because people think of it in a certain way, is a form of bourgeois thinking. It assumes that the construction of *races*, and thus racism, is primarily a formal problem of the natural sciences, rather than a social phenomenon.

This is opposed by a historical-materialist concept of racism. It assumes that people's consciousness does not exist independently of the social conditions under which people live. Ideologies are therefore not random or arbitrary, but the product of social conditions. This means that not only racism itself emerges from social conditions, but also the idealist concept of racism, which reduces it to a problem of consciousness or fallacy. Consequently, both racism and liberal anti-racism are "objective forms of thought" and products of bourgeois society (Marx, 1996: 87). The most crucial premise of a historical-materialist critique of racism is therefore that it can only be understood through its social and historical conditions. The critique of racism from the perspective of Marxist anti-racism thus always has political consequences, because this understanding has the concrete purpose of abolishing it. Therefore, this article presents a concept of racism that is characterized by its historical development in the context of social relations of production, exploitation and violence.[1]

1   The Capitalist Mode of Production and Racism

In everyday consciousness, racism is often perceived as an inherent aspect of all cultures and regions of the world, a quasi-natural reaction to the foreign. This ahistorical assumption, which views racism as an anthropological constant, is countered by a materialist understanding. Racism must be understood in its historical becoming and development.

The anti-colonial Marxist tradition posits that the emergence of racism is contingent upon the capitalist mode of production. It asserts that primarily material interests rather than a racist ideology of inequality between Europeans and "others" are the primary driving force behind colonialism and enslavement.[2] As Walter Rodney observed: "Occasionally, there is a misunderstanding

---

[1] The level of abstraction and the limited capacity of this text mean that certain aspects, such as gender relations, which are not insignificant to the issue at hand, are analytically excluded. The specific entanglement of racism, class relations and patriarchal relations, which makes the social position of non-white and migrant women a specific one that cannot be subsumed under racialization and class alone. See the contribution by Eleonora Roldán Mendívil and Hannah Vögele in this volume, pp. 36–50.

[2] Based on the reception of literature that primarily refers to the tradition of anti-colonial Marxism and originates from the US-American and Caribbean region as well as from the

that Europeans enslaved Africans for racist reasons (Rodney, 2018: 103)." Similarly, Eric Williams posited that "slavery was not born of racism: rather, racism was born of slavery (Williams, 1994: 33)."

2 Colonialism as "Original Accumulation"

According to the US historian Winthrop Jordan, the pre-colonial encounters between English travelers, merchants and Africans were not primarily characterized by racist prejudices and their counterparts were not imagined as slaves (Jordan, 2003: 33). Although there were pre-colonial negative representations of Africans that may have facilitated colonial subjugation (Miles and Brown, 2003: 133), the relevant question in this context is whether these are sufficient to explain racist and colonial relations and ultimately violence. If we understand racism as more than just a prejudice against "the other," but as a social relation between people, this statement is not sufficient. The condition of possibility for the emergence of racist ideologies must therefore be sought where people are placed in relation to one another.

With the emergence of the capitalist world market, a global context develops in which different regions of the earth are no longer understood as distinct, self-contained worlds. A coherent world order emerges that is not held together by a homogeneous culture or an all-encompassing political system, but by the global division of labor in the capitalist mode of production (Wallerstein, 2004: 24). The analysis of racism therefore begins with the historical onset of the capitalist mode of production.

> The discovery of gold and silver in America, the extirpation, enslavement and entombment in mines of the aboriginal population, the beginning of the conquest and looting of the East Indies, the turning of Africa into a warren for the commercial hunting of black-skins, signalised the rosy dawn of the era of capitalist production.
> MARX, 1996, 739

The so-called *original accumulation*, the accumulation of the first capital, was not, as bourgeois economists claimed, a process that was linked to the thrift and rationality of the first capitalists, but was based on violent expropriation.

African continent, I refer in the following to anti-black/anti-African colonial racism as an example.

In Europe, among other things, communal property was converted into private property, rural populations were expropriated and forced into wage labor, sometimes under life-threatening conditions. A decisive moment of the so-called original accumulation was the colonial system: "The treasures captured outside Europe by undisguised looting, enslavement, and murder, floated back to the mother-country and were there turned into capital (Ibid: 741)."

The European colonizers were motivated by a desire for land that could be cultivated, in natural resources and products, and in labor. In the Americas, a number of factors led to the necessity of procuring labor from other colonies, including: The indigenous population's superior knowledge of the land, which gave them a position of power over the colonizers, and the enormous decimation of the indigenous population caused by the brutal behavior of the colonial conquerors and the diseases they brought with them from Europe quickly required a supply of cheap and subservient labor (Geulen, 2007: 39–40). Hence, people were abducted from the African continent and enslaved in order to extract natural resources and produce goods for the European metropoles.³

3   Colonial Super-exploitation of Labor

The form of production imposed on the colonies and the form of labor, i.e. slavery, differed from those in the European metropole, where wage labor was dominant. Nevertheless, the mode of production in the colonies was neither feudal nor pre-bourgeois, but already capitalist. Slavery as unfree labor and "free" wage labor are both capitalist forms of labor that stand in relation to one another: "In fact, the veiled slavery of the wage workers in Europe needed, for its pedestal, slavery pure and simple in the new world (Marx, 1996: 747)." The sharp distinction between slavery and wage labor also excludes the violent nature of wage labor in Europe: "The decline in direct violence associated with 'free labor' was the result of decades of struggle and the realization by capitalists that the persistent problems with labor discipline could not be solved by enslavement (Frings, 2019: 431)."

At the advent of the nascent capitalist mode of production, workers in the metropoles also labored under similarly poor conditions as the colonized (Cox,

---

3   C.f. Cox (2003, 71–78). An obvious thesis here is that, as a lesson from the problems with the Native Americans, the people from Africa were deliberately herded together from different regions and different ethnic groups with different languages in order to disorganize them and deprive them of the opportunity to resist.

2003: 73). Indeed, workdays of 16 to 20 hours and wages below the subsistence level, that is, general impoverishment, were pervasive. These conditions constituted the initial impetus for labor struggles that sought to improve working conditions, including the establishment of the standard eight-hour workday. These struggles contributed to the emergence of a civilization characterized by exploitative conditions in factories (Marx, 1996: ch. 8). The historical level that allows workers to engage in cultural reproduction and leisure activities in addition to mere survival is a consequence of class struggles and the realization by capitalists that with improved working conditions, the rate of exploitation can remain high.

The conditions of production established in the colony and the social relations of power and domination differ from those in the metropole. In the colony, the relations of exploitation appear to be congruent with the colonial relations of violence. As a result, labor struggles that seek to improve working conditions as such and directly relate to an economic clash of interests have rarely developed there. For the colonized, the colonial relations of violence and oppression often appear to be the actual relationship of exploitation that they are struggling against. Frantz Fanon highlights this distinction in *The Wretched of the Earth*, emphasizing that the anti-colonial struggle, which primarily addresses colonial political rule, must not replace the social struggle over property relations and the organization of society (Fanon, 1963: 143). Consequently, the distinction between the colony and the metropole entails disparate starting conditions for the struggles of workers in Europe and in the colonies. The differential legal status of colonial workers and the inferior standard of living provided an opportunity for the super-exploitation of African labor. European workers earned far more than African workers, with some of them being paid below the subsistence level (Rodney, 2018: 176–77).

In this case, super-exploitation does not denote a state of exception, but rather a relation that is a cornerstone of capitalist accumulation. Exploitation is a defining feature of all class societies. The specific feature of wage labor is that, unlike slavery or serfdom, it does not involve an immediate personal property relationship. Rather, the lack of ownership of the means of production forces the majority of the population into dependence on capital. People are forced into wage labor, which is to say, they are compelled to sell their labor power as a commodity. Unlike in previous class societies, in which a slave had a specific master or a peasant had to pay taxes to a specific lord, there are no specific individuals facing each other but classes stand in relation to each other. The wages paid to the workers are determined by the cost of reproducing their labor power rather than by the value they create. The difference between the produced output and the remuneration paid to the worker represents the surplus value that the capitalists appropriate. Capital is therefore not simply a thing, but the constant movement of the appropriation of surplus labor by capitalists. Super-exploitation is a phenomenon that combines the general conditions of production with the particular: an intensified exploitation of labor power. This can be achieved either by paying a lower wage in relation to the social average or the socially negotiated minimum or by extending working hours beyond the limits of the standard working day. Such super-exploitation can be institutionalized through laws by granting only certain sections of the working class the right to social protection.

In this context, racism within the colonial relations of production functioned primarily as an instrument of domination, assigning social positions to people through the use of *race* ideology. By naturalizing certain characteristics such as inferiority, lack of culture and low intelligence in connection with physical resilience in the colonized, the ruling class in Europe was able to relegate them to a certain position within the relations of production. As whites, Europeans perceived themselves as complementary in their characteristics and thus as predestined to manage and organize production (Miles and Brown, 2003: 124).

4 Formal Analysis of Colonial Racism

Although the content of these attributions fulfills a concrete political function, it also results from the working conditions themselves. Racism can be defined as an objective form of thought in the relation between exploitation and super-exploitation. The condition for the emergence of racist ideology is the unequal development of political relations between the European metropole and the colonies. In the colony, the relation of economic exploitation appears, as already mentioned, to be congruent with the relation of political violence.

The starting point is the illusory nature of the bourgeois principles of freedom and equality. Freedom and equality are illusory insofar as they are valid in the sphere of circulation, i.e. on the market, but not in the sphere of production. The exploitation of workers in capitalism is facilitated by the contradiction between the exchange of wages and labor. The purchase of labor power by capitalists is not an equal exchange because, as previously stated, workers are not compensated for the entirety of their labor. Instead, they are paid a wage that is sufficient for survival and, depending on their social status, for cultural and domestic reproduction. The concept of freedom refers to the double freedom of wage laborers in Europe: On the one hand, it implies the ability to be unbound and legally entitled to do so. On the other hand, it also implies a lack of property and the economic compulsion to sell one's labor power for wages. Equality, on the other hand, is contingent upon the law of exchange, which requires that equal values be exchanged between two individuals who are both free and equal legal subjects. However, the appearance of freedom and equality that exists for workers in Europe through the postulated human rights and bourgeois constitutions dissolves in the colony. In the colony, open exploitation and open relations of violence prevail. The discrepancy between the principles of universal human rights and the actual working and living conditions in the colonies, which are characterized by inequality, violence and super-exploitation, necessitates ideological rationalization. This glaring contradiction is constitutive of racism (Schmitt-Egner, 1978: 361–70).

The limitation of working hours, such as the standard eight-hour working day, which was fought for in the metropole, did not apply in the colony. The colonized were required to work far beyond that. As a result, the value of their labor was below the value of labor determined by the social average in the European metropole. According to Schmitt-Egner, this inferiorized them literally (Ibid: 367). Due to the low value of labor, the use of machines was not worthwhile, so that the colonized had to perform unskilled manual labor far below the historical-technical level of the time. As a result, they were considered underdeveloped: "It is clear to the racist that the cheap labor, whatever nation, culture or race they may come from, has not yet made the step to becoming a Central European civilized man (Ruf, 1989: 78)." In addition, many skilled workers who had been trained in the (former) colonies migrated to the industrial centers because the low wages there were paid there were still higher than the wages in their home countries. This phenomenon is known as a "brain drain" from these parts of the world (Rodney, 2018: 21).

Furthermore, the wages of non-enslaved colonized people were sometimes paid in food rather than money (Schmitt-Egner, 1978: 378). This meant that the colonized did not participate in the market as free exchangers and were therefore not granted the central moment of equality in bourgeois society as free members of the exchange process. They were therefore also not regarded as bourgeois subjects. On the one hand, because almost all indigenous political, social and cultural institutions were destroyed during the colonization process. On the other hand, because the cultural aspect of life, specifically everything that goes beyond mere survival, which should also be covered by wages, was omitted. They were thus reduced to their physical preservation and therefore to their nature. In bourgeois society, where human subjectivity is determined by the difference between nature and culture (Horkheimer and Adorno, 2002), colonized people are no longer regarded as human beings due to their supposed lack of culture, but as quasi-animal beings.

It can be added here that the ideology of inferiority, which arose due to the reduction to natural reproduction, also applied to the working class in the metropole. The European bourgeoisie felt a similar contempt for the working class as for members of the inferior *races*. In some cases, they were also described as an inferior *race* with low intelligence (Miles, 1999: 12).[4] In this context, the question therefore arises as to how this economic difference, the super-exploitation of colonial labor, gives rise to racist ideology.

5   Racism as Ideology

Racism as an ideology is meant to rationalize and justify economic inequality. In order to convince society, it requires the introduction of extra-economic factors to explain this difference. In the case of colonial racism, the most obvious and literal differences serve as markers of difference. Skin color appears as the form of difference that is experienced and validated socially. It also enables ideological transfiguration because Manichaeism (Christian color symbolism) can be utilized to further rationalize difference. The color white is perceived as divine, good, and innocent, while black is associated with evil, devilishness, and sinfulness. These characteristics can be projected onto the colonized, transforming Africans into Blacks and Europeans into Whites (Fanon, 1963: 6).

The process of racial construction is inherently dialectical. When defining and classifying "the others," the self, one's own identity, is also constructed. "The African's 'blackness' therefore reflected the European's 'whiteness': these opposites were bound together, each giving meaning to the other in a totality of signification (Miles and Brown, 2003: 101)." Accordingly, we can understand racial identity constructions as a social relation in which neither side can exist without the other.

In light of Marx's observations on the fetish, we may consider the social mediation of these categories. The process of racialization and the construction of racist categories renders *race*, which is a man-made category and economically produced difference, as a natural difference. One may analogize the mediation between economic position and *race* to the fetishism of money. The fact that dark skin did not necessarily imply enslavement does not negate the fact that the enslaved were all of dark skin, which led to the perception

---

4   The parallels between class chauvinism and racism cannot be discussed here, but it is also relevant for our thesis to note that racial research in England began in the working class: "Research into 'race' in Britain arose in connection with concerns about the lack of intelligence of the working class (Terkessidis, 2017)."

of a natural difference that was experienced and validated socially (Chang, 1985: 42). The construction of *race* is a construction of skin color as a carrier of meaning. In skin color, a social relationship is reified.

This section dealt with the emergence of colonial racism and *race* ideology based on the expansion of capitalism.[5] The emergence of racist identity categories and the violence related to them, as well as their ideological independence, were derived from colonial relations of production. In the next section, this will be outlined using the example of the new racism in German immigration society to elaborate the specific racism against migrants in Germany based on these parallels.

6   Labor Migration and the New Racism in the Immigration Society

The old racism, which was based on biological *races*, has now largely given way to a new racism (Balibar and Wallerstein, 1988: 20). This differentiating or cultural racism no longer emphasizes racial hierarchies, but differences between cultures (Müller, 1992: 24–44; Hall, 1994). The category of immigration has replaced the category of *race*, so that it is now a "racism without races (Hall, 2000: 7–16)." In his 1988 essay "Is there a 'neo-racism'?" Étienne Balibar describes its two causes: Firstly, the old anti-racism had refuted the existence of *races*, so that racism had to find new forms of articulation. However, the most significant factor contributing to the emergence of the new racism was the reaction to the increased migration to the European metropoles. While in the era of colonialism, the migration flows of settlers led from Europe to the colonies, they have now reversed after formal decolonization and the formerly colonized subjects are migrating to Europe (Balibar and Wallerstein, 1988: 19–20).

Although Germany experienced less post-colonial migration than the other major European powers due to the revocation of its colonies after World War I, there was nevertheless increased migration from the periphery. The human casualties in World War II, the subsequent economic boom and the development of the Bundeswehr led to a labor shortage in the Federal Republic, which could no longer be compensated for (cheaply enough) by the domestic population alone (Nikolinakos, 1973: 25–36). From the 1950s onwards, recruitment agreements were signed with Italy (1955), Spain (1960), Greece (1960), Turkey

---

5   This can provide a basis for an analysis of neo-colonial/imperialist relations of production between leading industrialized nations and African states today and their consequences for the continuity of colonial racism. However, this analysis cannot take place in this article.

(1961), Morocco (1963), Portugal (1964), Tunisia (1965) and Yugoslavia (1968) in order to compensate for the labor shortage with so-called Gastarbeiter (guest workers).[6] The hiring of foreign labor was particularly suitable because, according to the Confederation of German Employers' Associations, "labor market requirements could be adjusted upwards and downwards (Nikolinakos, 1973: 68)." This means that there were "guest workers" who could be laid off depending on market conditions or used as a reserve. This was institutionalized through legislation and the so-called Inländerprimat (primacy of 'domestic' workers).[7]

German capital was thus able to achieve its primary objective of increasing profits by reducing the wage average. This was made possible by increased competition in the labor market and a consistently high number of unemployed individuals. They are always willing to work for less money because they are dependent on these jobs. They form a so-called industrial reserve army (Marx, 1996: 623–34). If the increased labor supply does not exist in this form, then labor must be imported through forms of migration.[8]

Here too, super-exploitation – through lower wages and worse working conditions – is the starting point for racialization. The experiences of "guest workers" from Turkey are exemplary. The accommodation in dormitories on the factory premises, the lack of privacy and the "barrack-like regulations, which often violated the normal freedoms of adult men (Jamin, 1999: 158)" were perceived as unpleasant by many migrants. Consequently, many lived without their families at first and had to significantly reduce their consumption (Ibid: 162). They were employed in factories, where they were limited to physical reproduction.

A superficial and vulgar view suggests that racism arises because migrant workers had the function of depressing the wages of domestic workers. However, the thesis of the *wage-depressing function of guest workers* is a right-wing argument that has been falsely generalized. On the contrary, the recruitment of

---

6 There were "first and second class" agreements: In contrast to the agreements with Morocco, Tunisia and Turkey, those with Italy, Portugal and Spain had no restrictions on family reunification and the length of stay. Due to the economic benefits for migrants and a statement by the Confederation of German Employers' Associations, which condemned the rotation principle as costly and ineffective, the regulations were later relaxed for the other sending states. Cf. Jamin (1999: 149–150).

7 Recruitment ended in 1973, but the state-organized recruitment of migrant workers is no longer necessary anyway. In many sectors, labor shortages can be compensated for by family reunification, refugees and other migrants without explicit state recruitment. Cf. Diettrich (1999).

8 Another option would be to relocate production to areas with lower average wages (Ruf, 1989: 73). An example of this is the relocation of the textile industry to South Asia.

"guest workers" has enabled upward social mobility for German workers, so that there is no direct competition between them. The competition between German unskilled workers and "guest workers" arises only when trade unions have no influence on wage policy. This suggests that German workers have a general interest in employing foreign workers in low-skilled jobs (Nikolinakos, 1973: 95). Consequently, there may be different attitudes towards migrant workers among the different segments of the labor market and therefore of the working class. While higher-level workers have an interest in employing foreign labor as long as they serve as a downward buffer, unskilled workers are in direct competition with them.

In addition to super-exploitation by capital, migrants develop a sense of inferiority resulting from being forced into low-skilled jobs that are considered inferior by society. According to Werner Ruf, many migrants compensate for this with a higher work ethic in order to prove themselves, which further contributes to competition in the workplace (Ruf, 1989: 79). Such competition is conducive to the breeding of racist resentment, given that migrant workers work harder for less money. Although they are merely attempting to compensate for their competitive disadvantage, German workers perceive them as the cause of their impending social decline and falling wages (Ibid: 80).

The thesis of the wage-depressing function does not hold up to scrutiny whereas the buffer function thesis appears more conclusive. According to calculations by migration researcher Friedrich Heckmann, 2.3 million Germans have moved into white-collar positions (Heckmann, 1981; Karakayali, 2008: 104). Racism against migrants is thus more "linked to the relative privileges of qualification, to the difference between exploitation and super-exploitation (Balibar and Wallerstein, 1988: 224)."

7   Racism and Crisis

Despite pre-existing racism and a tradition of German nationalism, even in post-National Socialist West Germany, tensions between Germans and migrants came to a head in the 1980s and especially after 1989 (Jamin, 1999: 160). The violent racism that developed during this period cannot be attributed solely to the presence of migrants, as they had been in Germany for decades at that time.

> It should be noted that it was only in the 1970s, especially since the increase in family reunification following the recruitment stop in 1973, that large numbers of Turks went from being isolated exotic housing residents to becoming part of the normal resident population, competing

with Germans for housing and being present in schools and other public institutions.
Ibid: 160–61

It can be observed that the phenomenon of racist violence is linked to crises (Balibar and Wallerstein, 1988: 217). This was particularly evident in Germany in the 1980s. Racist violence against migrants and media discourses with inflammatory language such as "The boat is full" crystallized at this time. In order to understand the nature of this racist crisis, it is necessary to view it in the social and historical context in which it occurred, which includes a parallel economic and political crisis. The recruitment stop occurred in the context of the 1973 oil price crisis, which was the worst recession since World War II for Western industrialized countries. In the 1990s, at the height of racist violence, the capitalist restoration of East Germany and general impoverishment and declassification in the new states of Germany were additional crisis factors.

While in 1972 the two millionth guest worker, a Portuguese woman, had been welcomed by the President of the Federal Employment Agency and the Bavarian Minister of Labor and presented with champagne, flowers and a portable television, the presence of immigrant workers was immediately problematized in the wake of the crisis in the 1980s. Contrary to expectations, however, the recruitment stop did result in an increased return of "guest workers" to the sending countries, but instead they settled in Germany, leading to increased family reunification. Thus, they became part of German society, which now had to come to terms with its reality as a country of immigration[9] and not merely as a country of residence. Max Frisch (2005) wrote about this turning point in 1965: "We wanted workers, but human beings came." In addition, an increasing number of refugees arrived in Germany from the mid-1980s onwards.

The social relationship between immigrants and Germans has become one in which competition is permitted on the job market, in housing, in schools, and for social participation. This competitive relationship provides bourgeois politics with the opportunity to racially rationalize social problems such as homelessness, crime and social declassification in times of crisis (Balibar and Wallerstein, 1988: 220). The coincidence of the crisis with increased immigration suggests a causal link between the racist discourse against immigrants and the presence of immigrants in the face of social problems. During this phase,

---

9   There has always been migration to Germany and it has also been common for various migrants from Eastern Europe or the former colonies to stay in Germany.

the well-known right-wing slogan "Deutschland den Deutschen, Ausländer raus" (Germany to the Germans, foreigners out) becomes popular. The main objective is to gain a competitive advantage in terms of (supposedly) limited resources through racist exclusions.

Increased family reunification and the integration of the second generation into schools also create social problems that give rise to a political discourse on integration. In order to promote educational integration of second-generation immigrants, special education classes and classes for foreigners are being established. This leads to a social segregation of immigrant children from German children. The integration debate is also spreading to other areas of society, and immigrants are accused of living in parallel societies and not adapting to German values and legal norms. This creates a paradox in the demand for integration, especially with regard to the following generations of immigrants:

> [T]he less the population designated by the category of immigration is effectively "immigrant," that is, foreign, not only by its status and social function, but also in its customs and culture, the more it is denounced as a foreign body.
> Ibid: 223

Cultural foreignness, therefore, appears to be a surface-level issue. A connection between racialization and class can be established here. Just as there are positive references to well-qualified and educated immigrants in many supposedly non-racist arguments, there is also resentment against upwardly mobile immigrants: "Turkish cleaning ladies are easier to tolerate than Syrian dermatologists (Castro, 2015: 92)."

> The failure to recognize the economic foundations and the political-economic connections of the employment of foreigners leads to the fact that the latest efforts to 'integrate' guest workers mentioned at the beginning run the risk of perpetuating the discrimination of guest workers and maintaining the mechanism of exploitation to which they are exposed.
> NIKOLINAKOS, 1973: 11–12

The rationale behind this phenomenon can be elucidated by the aforementioned buffer function of immigrant workers. It appears that immigrants are only desired as long as they remain in their designated social position. As soon as immigrants experience upward social mobility, step out of their assigned position and enter into a direct competitive relationship with Germans, interest in their employment transforms into resentment. Following the cessation of recruitment and subsequent reunification, immigrants were compelled to demonstrate their self-employment in order to avoid deportation. Consequently, many resorted to illegality or became small business owners (Bojadžijev, 2012: 237). This illustrates the contradictory aspect of racism: while the immigrants' foreignness is problematized and absolute adaptation to German society is demanded, this very behavior is sanctioned in the form of racist resentment.

This analysis posits that the social inequality between racialized foreigners and Germans and the racism directed at the former cannot be understood in terms of a mere continuity of colonial racism or a shift in the articulation of racist discourse. As the subjects who have been racialized have changed, so too has the racism that rationalized colonialism. The racism that justified the super-exploitation of immigrants under Fordism is not the same as that which rationalized colonialism. A comparable analysis of neoliberal racism has yet to be done.

In the following section, the two historical forms of racism described here will be used to develop what they mean for a political-theoretical definition of racism and what constitutes a historical-materialist concept of racism.

8 A Historical-Materialist Concept of Racism

In place of racism, the terms xenophobia or hostility towards foreigners are often employed to describe the new racism. "The distinction between racism and xenophobia [serves] to differentiate between attacks on and discrimination against 'blacks' and 'immigrants (Ibid: 28).'" However, this sharp conceptual distinction between biologistic and culturalist racism does not hold up in the context of a historical-materialist concept of racism. The concept of xenophobia also attempts to distinguish between *race* as a socially constructed category and immigrants as a natural category, without addressing the conditions under which these categories are produced: "For as long as the group of immigrants exists, it only exists under conditions that make it such (Ibid: 15)." Even if the new racism does not explicitly argue with *race*, biological arguments return again and again. This was most clearly exemplified by the widely discussed theses of former SPD senator of finance Thilo Sarrazin, who used the differing birth rates of immigrant groups and Germans as well as IQ tests to promote a culture war rhetoric. With statements such as "I don't have to recognize anyone who depends on the state, rejects the state, doesn't take proper care of their children's education and constantly produces new little headscarf girls (Sarrazin, 2009: 199)," culture and ancestry became a general racist devaluation of immigrants, combined with a rationalization of socially produced class differences. Likewise, in racial theories, culture plays a non-negligible role. Culturalist arguments justifying colonialism were based on the premise that the colonized were inherently barbaric and underdeveloped. This justification was used to justify the exploitation of colonized populations (Balibar and Wallerstein, 1988: 21). Culturalism and biologism are both components of racism, which can move between these poles in its arguments, but ultimately asserts a static identity of body and culture (Müller, 1992). It equates the social form of labor, reified through physical or cultural characteristics, with human nature. Social hierarchization is thus rendered natural.

Despite the non-existence of biological *races* or clearly definable cultural groups, the principle of racialization is not arbitrary. Belonging to a racialized group is determined by the temporal and spatial location of integration into capitalist production as labor (Paolucci, 2006: 642). Immanuel Wallerstein (1983: 77) therefore also describes racism as the "ethnicization of the world work-force." This also explains the extent to which racism is a modern phenomenon that has to do with the development of the capitalist mode of production. The creation of a global market for raw materials and labor and, as a result, the super-exploitation of the colonized and immigrants are the conditions for the emergence of racism. It is therefore a social relation between people who are included and exploited in the production process in different ways. Racism takes place within social contexts, specifically within the capitalist mode of production (Chang, 1985: 39).

Racism can therefore have a functional moment in capitalism. By ideologically transfiguring the super-exploitation of a group of labor, social relations are naturalized: "Thus, racism was not simply a legitimation of class exploitation. It represented the social world in a way that identified a specific population as a labouring class (Miles and Brown, 2003: 124)." European workers and the petty bourgeoisie in particular can make use of racist ideologies in the face of potential social declassification, which is pervasive in class society, because the supposedly only thing that prevents them from sinking to the lowest level of the social hierarchy is the maintenance of the *racial barrier* (Schmitt-Egner, 1978: 381). The working class is materially differentiated and hierarchized by relative privilege and the distinction between exploitation and super-exploitation (Balibar and Wallerstein, 1988: 224). By identifying with racist ideology and the superiority formulated therein, the working class is also politically de-solidarized. Racism thus functions as a "solvent of 'class consciousness (Ibid: 20).'"

However, ideology can also transact and become independent to the extent that it loses its political functionality for the capitalist mode of production

(Hund, 2015: 32). There is no functional or rational moment in racist violence and ultimately in genocide. The manner in which racism organizes compassion and empathy can be observed not least in the way that racist violence is dealt with. In the 1990s, racist violence in reunified Germany reached a peak with pogroms against immigrants. In 1992, the so-called Sonnenblumenhaus in Rostock-Lichtenhagen, an apartment block housing mostly Vietnamese immigrants, was attacked by right-wingers with Molotov cocktails, set on fire on one day and continued to be attacked for several more. The residents remained trapped in the building. Meanwhile, many German bystanders prevented the rescue teams from passing through and applauded the arsonists (Jüttner, 2007).

The pre-categorization of German and foreign workers in the context of omnipresent competition gives rise to crisis racism. This phenomenon is exemplified by the discussions surrounding the Herero and Nama in what is now Namibia, then German South-West Africa, during the period of German colonialism. In 1904, General Lothar von Trotha replaced Theodor Leutwein as military commander-in-chief. At the urging of the settlers, Trotha was preparing a *race* war. His predecessor Leutwein, however, preferred a milder course of action because the Herero could continue to be of economic use to the Germans as "small cattle breeders and especially as workers (Zimmerer, 2014)." Ultimately, the genocide of the Herero and Nama ensued and could not even be prevented by the similarly dehumanizing rational-economic considerations. This demonstrates that racism must be understood as an independent and contradictory phenomenon that cannot be derived solely from the needs of capital; rather it develops a momentum of its own.

It is evident that capitalism is not color-blind, as it relies on the exploitation of a section of the working class and the ideological legitimization thereof. For capital, however, racial violence is about the destruction of labor and thus the most important basis of capital accumulation. This is why difference and equality must always be balanced under capitalism. This dialectic of exploitation and extermination is essentially characteristic of racist formations. In order to comprehend the twofold nature of racism, it is essential to grasp both the economic basis of exploitation and the ideological rationalization that justifies it.

The various forms of racism must be examined in light of concrete historical examples, as there is no supra-historical concept of racism that aligns with a historical-materialist understanding of racism. However, as demonstrated here, some structural features can be identified that allow for a more abstract concept of racism.

While the relationship between exploitation and super-exploitation, which is expressed in racism as a social relation, exists materially and is real, it is only distorted in racist ideology as a relationship between *races* or cultures. On the one hand, racism expresses an abstract relation in social production and, on the other, it ideologically expresses the supposed overcoming of class positions through identification with *race* or culture instead of the economic and political class position. Stuart Hall addressed this contradiction by defining *race* as a psychological category through which the racialized experience their own class oppression:

> Racism is not only directed 'from the outside' against those whom it disposes and disarticulates (silences). It is also effective within the dominated subjects – those subordinate ethnic groups or 'races' who experience their relationship to their real conditions of existence and their domination by the ruling classes in and through the imaginary notions of racist invocation and who are made to experience themselves as 'the inferiors,' les autres. And yet these processes themselves are never exempt from the ideological class struggle.
> HALL, 2000: 136

9   Conclusion

This article examines the emergence of racism from the economic relations of production and its reproduction as a material structure. While it does not address psychological factors and the resulting problems in depth, it is important to recognize that they play a significant role. In *Black Skin, White Masks*, Frantz Fanon presents these psychological aspects of racism as a process of alienation brought about by social conditions. He argues that it cannot be abolished within bourgeois society (Fanon, 2008: xv). An understanding of the social preconditions and the material structure of racism is therefore the basis for such a debate. The relation between subject and society must be understood as one of interdependence. This article has attempted to present one aspect of this, the material side. An analysis and understanding of class society in capitalism is essential for comprehending the emergence and functioning of racism. By examining the categories that racism refers to, be it *race* or culture, it becomes evident that they are social relations that refer to relations of production. This analytical basis allows for the critical examination of contemporary forms of dominant anti-racism.

If racism is regarded as a problem of subjective attitudes, we remain at the level of the individual. In this view, structural racism would then be defined as the totality of the racist attitudes of people in a given society. This perspective is consistent with the prevailing ideology of liberalism, which does not understand society as a relation between people, but only as the sum of individuals. This perspective, which is pervasive in the field of racism research, carries the risk of transforming social conditions into the intentional actions of subjects. This, in turn, leads to the view that racism is solely a matter of consciousness. Marx, in *The German Ideology*, already observed that such an attitude is, in fact, an affirmation of material conditions: "This demand to change consciousness amounts to a demand to interpret the existing world in a different way, i.e., to recognise it by means of a different interpretation (Marx, 1976: 30)."

In contrast, a materialist concept of racism posits that racism, or at least its condition of existence, is located in the material structure of society. Racist difference does not become articulated through explicitly racist actions, but is already articulated economically through social inequality. A political strategy that aims to combat racism without taking class relations into account must seek to achieve a proportional distribution of racialized people in the respective classes within the existing relations, because it is not the relationship of exploitation as such that is problematized, but merely the disproportionately high distribution of racialized individuals in certain class positions (Reed Jr, 2013: 53–56).

The question is not merely whether anti-racism, which is indispensable in view of the racist violence of the last century, can be content with equality within the existing conditions. A materialist concept of racism calls into question whether this is possible at all. Any anti-racism that is limited to addressing racism on an ideological level, whether by challenging the existence of biological races or implementing an anti-prejudice pedagogy, is ultimately futile unless it also addresses the underlying relations of exploitation and their social preconditions.

Bibliography

Balibar, Ètienne and Immanuel Wallerstein (1988) *Race Nation Class*. Ambiguous Identities. London and New York: Verso.

Bojadžijev, Manuela (2012) *Die windige Internationale. Rassismus und Kämpfe der Migration*. Münster: Dampfboot Verlag.

Castro, Mario Varela (2015) Willkommenskultur: Rassismus und Ökonomie. In Çetin Zülfukar and Savaş Taş (eds.), *Gespräche über Rassismus*. Berlin: Yilmaz-Günay, Koray.

Chang, Harry (1985) Toward a Marxist Theory of Racism: Two Essays by Harry Chang, *Review of Radical Political Economics*, vol. 17, no. 3, pp. 34–45, DOI: 10.1177/048661348501700303.

Cox, Oliver C. (2003) "Race Relations" in Les Back and John Solomos (eds.), *Theories of Race and Racism. A Reader*. London: Routledge.

Diettrich, Ben (1999) *Klassenfragmentierung im Postfordismus: Geschlecht, Arbeit, Rassismus, Marginalisierung*. Münster: Unrast Verlag.

Fanon, Frantz (2008) *Black Skin White Masks*. New York: Pluto Press.

Fanon, Frantz (1963) *The Wretched of the Earth*. New York: Grove Press.

Frings, Christian (2019) Sklaverei und Lohnarbeit bei Marx, *Prokla*, vol. 3, pp. 427–48.

Frisch, Max (2005) Der Schweizer Schriftsteller Max Frisch 1965 zum Thema Immigration "… und es kommen Menschen," *Berliner Zeitung*, Jan 1, berliner-zeitung.de/15652010.

Geulen, Christian (2007) *Geschichte des Rassismus*. München: C.H. Beck.

Hall, Stuart (2000) Rassismus als Ideologischer Diskurs. In Nora Räthzel (ed.), *Theorien über Rassismus*. Hamburg: Argument Verlag.

Hall, Stuart (1994) *Rassismus und Kulturelle Identität. Ausgewählte Schriften 2*. Hamburg: Argument Verlag.

Heckmann, Friedrich (1981) *Die Bundesrepublik – ein Einwanderungsland? Zur Soziologie der Gastarbeiterbevölkerung als Einwandererminorität*. Stuttgart: Klett-Cotta, as cited in Serhat Karakayali (2008), *Gespenster der Migration. Zur Genealogie illegaler Einwanderung in der Bundesrepublik Deutschland*. Bielefeld: transcript.

Horkheimer Max and Theodor W. Adorno (2002) *Dialectic of Enlightenment*. Stanford: Stanford University Press.

Hund, Wulf D. (2015) *Rassismus*. Bielefeld: Transcript Verlag.

Jamin, Mathilde (1999) Fremde Heimat. Zur Geschichte der Arbeitsmigration aus der Türkei. In Jan Motte et al. (eds.) *50 Jahre Bundesrepublik – 50 Jahre Einwanderung. Nachkriegsgeschichte als Migrationsgeschichte*. Frankfurt and New York: Campus Verlag.

Jordan, Wintrop D. (2003) First Impressions. In Les Back and John Solomos (eds.), *Theories of Race and Racism. A Reader*. London: Routledge.

Jüttner, Julia (2007) Rostock-Lichtenhagen Als der Mob die Herrschaft übernahm, *Spiegel Online*, August 23, spiegel.de/einestages/rostock-lichtenhagen-als-der-mob-die-herrschaft-uebernahm-a-946806.html.

Marx, Karl (1996) Capital: A Critique of Political Economy, Volume 1. In Karl Marx and Frederick Engels, *Collected Works Vol. 35*. London: Lawrence and Wishart.

Marx, Karl (1976) The German Ideology. In Karl Marx and Frederick Engels, *Collected Works Vol. 5*. London: Lawrence and Wishart.

Miles, Robert and Malcolm Brown (2003) *Racism*. London: Routledge.

Miles, Robert (1999) Geschichte des Rassismus. In Christoph Burgmer (ed.), *Rassismus in der Diskussion*. Berlin: Espresso Verlag.

Müller, Jost (1992) Rassismus und die Fallstricke des gewöhnlichen Antirassismus. In redaktion diskus (eds.), *Die freundliche Zivilgesellschaft. Rassismus und Nationalismus in Deutschland*. Berlin and Amsterdam: Edition ID-Archiv.

Nikolinakos, Marios (1973) *Politische Ökonomie der Gastarbeiterfrage. Migration und Kapitalismus*. Reinbek: Rowohlt Taschenbuch Verlag.

Paolucci, Paul (2006) Race and Racism in Marx's Camera Obscura, *Critical Sociology*, vol. 32, no. 4, pp. 617–648, DOI: 10.1163/156916306779155207.

Reed Jr, Adolph (2013) Marx, Race, and Neoliberalism, *New Labor Forum*, vol. 22, no. 1, pp. 49–57, DOI: 10.1177/1095796012471637.

Rodney, Walter (2018) *How Europe Underdeveloped Africa*. London: Verso.

Ruf, Werner (1989) Rassismus und Ökonomie. In Otger Autara et al., *Theorien über Rassismus. Eine Tübinger Veranstaltungsreihe*. Hamburg: Argument Verlag, pp. 63–84.

Sarrazin, Thilo (2009) Klasse statt Masse. Von der Hauptstadt der Transferleistungen zur Metropole der Eliten, *Interview by Lettre International*, vol. 86.

Schmitt Egner, Peter (1978) Wertgesetz und Rassismus. Zur begrifflichen Genesis kolonialer und faschistischer Bewusstseinsformen, *Gesellschaft. Beiträge zur Marxschen Theorie*, vol. 8/9, pp. 350–405.

Terkessidis, Mark (2017) Da war doch was? Über Rassismus reden, *TAZ*, Feb 20, taz.de/!5382405/.

Wallerstein, Immanuel (1983) *Historical Capitalism*. London: Verso.

Wallerstein, Immanuel (2004) *World-Systems Analysis. An Introduction*. Durham and London: Duke University Press.

Williams, Eric (1994) *Capitalism & Slavery*. Chapel Hill: The University of North Carolina Press.

Zimmerer, Jürgen (2014) Widerstand und Genozid: Der Krieg des Deutschen Reiches gegen die Herero (1904–1908), *bpd.de*, June 20, bpb.de/apuz/186874/widerstand-und-genozid-der-krieg-des-deutschen-reiches-gegen-die-herero.

CHAPTER 3

Social Reproduction, Gender, and Racism

Eleonora Roldán Mendívil and Hannah Vögele

The question of social reproduction, that is, the production of life, is central to any understanding of social relations (of production). This is where, among other things, the gendered division of labor and thus specific gender attributions are manifested. Globally, it is disproportionately women and girls who take care of the household, education and nursing, often underpaid or unpaid. In society as a whole, the care of the young, the elderly and/or the sick is usually organized under precarious conditions of wage labor. This is the basis for the constant renewal of the capitalist source of surplus value: human labor. At the same time, this often takes place in an invisible social framework of the private sphere, which is sealed off from public life. The COVID-19 pandemic has briefly drawn attention to issues of healthcare and nursing in particular, emphasizing their centrality to social survival. However, this focus has quickly receded again behind the dominant desire to return to so-called normalcy. This crisis serves to highlight in an acute manner the vital importance of care, for example in nursing and domestic care, which is largely organized on the backs of women in order to – ideally quietly – keep the economy running. In a paradoxical manner, the significance of essential care for the operation of the economy is simultaneously acknowledged and denied, as evidenced, for instance, by the perpetuation of the separation of spheres and the failure to recognize the interconnectivity between them.

No production without the reproduction of life – that is the simplified assertion of social reproduction theories. In addition to the pandemic, the importance of focusing on the sphere of social reproduction has been highlighted in recent years by various intensified labor struggles in areas such as education and cleaning. For example, mass strike movements by teachers are flaring up around the world.[1] Many teachers are striking for the public good. In particular, this encompasses not only higher wages but also social support for students, opposition to racist school policies, and affordable housing, as was emphasized by the Chicago Teachers Union during its 2019 strike (Burns,

---

1   For example, in Peru in 2017, the United States in 2012, 2018, and 2019, in Chile in 2019, and in Germany in 2021.

2019). The struggles of cleaners such as Justice for Cleaners at SOAS University of London, the grassroots union of hotel cleaners Las Kellys in Spain or the cleaners of the Paris metro also demonstrate that education and cleaning are not apolitical areas of society. Rather, they illustrate that working conditions in these areas are also being renegotiated through constant class struggle. The women's strikes or feminist strikes that have spread globally in recent years, particularly from Latin America and Spain, seek to integrate the struggles for compensated and uncompensated reproductive labor and those at the sites of production with those against sexualized and gender-based violence (Ni Una Menos, 2018).

With regard to the organization of struggles that go beyond feminist and anti-racist demands, in this article we want to outline the potential of social reproduction theory for the analysis of contemporary capitalist societies. This is because questions of gender and the organization of life-sustaining work are often central to analyses of racism in particular, but are repeatedly excluded or not identified in a dialectical-historical materialist manner. How are systems and effects of exploitation and oppression mutually constitutive? Insofar as the connection between gender and *race* in capitalism is addressed at all, it is typically done by means of the concept of intersection nowadays.[2] A materialist analysis from the perspective of social reproduction makes it possible to prevent reductive understandings of these social relations. This is true whether the tendency is to formulate categories of oppression as additive and individualizing or as abstract juxtapositions, or whether the limited Marxist understanding is employed that explains gender relations only in terms of class relations. In this regard, we offer a concise overview of the origins of this feminist-Marxist current, without claiming to provide an exhaustive account of the broader debate.[3] Our objective is to provide impetus for the ongoing critique of racism. The second part of the article is primarily concerned with the manner in which social relations and sites of reproduction serve to perpetuate racist structures and, at the same time, have the potential to be a decisive factor in resistance to them, both historically and currently.

---

2   See the chapter by Eleonora Roldán Mendívil and Bafta Sarbo in this volume, pp. 66–79.
3   We draw mainly on Marxist-feminist discussions in Western countries in recent decades.

1   Relations of Reproduction

Social reproduction theory is an approach to develop a coherent Marxist-feminist understanding of everyday life under capitalism. Focusing on the banality of everyday life and how it is unequally preserved and promoted enables us to rethink the relation between exploitation and oppression. According to Tithi Bhattacharya (2017: 3), the theory of social reproduction deals with

> questions of oppression (gender, race, sexuality) in distinctly nonfunctionalist ways precisely because oppression is theorized as structurally relational to, and hence shaped by, capitalist production rather than on the margins of analysis or as add-ons to a deeper and more vital economic process.

The fundamental question that arises is this: "If workers' labor produces all the wealth in society, who then produces the worker (Ibid: 1)?" What occurs in the spaces and social relations between the workplace, home, school, hospital, nursing home, kindergarten, etc.? Who performs this work and under what conditions? And what role do these jobs play in the process of capitalist accumulation? After all, this sphere is maintained and produced by human labor.

To answer these questions, social reproduction theory draws attention to the contradictions and invisible economic spaces of an economic and political system that does not, or only partially, take into account the basic needs of its participants (Federici, 2012). This represents an important change in perspective. The focus now shifts to the forms of work that enable the satisfaction of the necessities of life, as well as to the actors involved (Jaffe, 2020). It is therefore about the reproduction of society as a whole, whereby the framework of social reproduction can act as a "key to developing a sufficiently dynamic understanding of the working class (Bhattacharya, 2017: 69)." This also expands a frequently held narrow view of workers and the working class itself. It consists not only of immediate wage laborers, but of all "past, present, and potential wage-labour force, together with all those whose maintenance depends on the wage but who do not or cannot themselves enter wage-labour (Vogel, 2013: 166)." This view undermines the divisive, false and yet still prevalent image of a purely white and male working class in the West. Feminist social movements and Marxist-feminist theory have challenged this notion since the 1970s (Hartmann, 1981; Arruzza, 2017). Today, after the hegemony of liberal feminism, materialist analyses of care and reproductive labor are becoming more visible again. Within the framework of these theoretical debates and practical struggles, it is possible to analyze the historical emergence of certain social relations in greater detail and formulate (class-based) political demands in relation to forms of work that are widely glorified as mere labor of love. Social reproduction plays an important role in maintaining the capitalist mode of production and the super-exploitation of racialized people, as well as those marked as female, and therefore also has the potential to contribute to the overthrow of society.

2 Social Reproduction Theory

Based on analyses of gender and capitalism in Marxist theory and socialist practice,[4] the gender question and the question of social reproduction were discussed in depth and comprehensively during the 1970s. In the preceding years, the work undertaken by women and the women's rights associated with it had been made visible more radically in the West and became an important moment of revolt in a radicalizing youth movement. This can be explained by the post-war prosperity of Western states and the easier and broader access of women to higher education. Today, the analyses developed at that time are being taken up again, applied to changed social circumstances and reformulated.

Many feminists of that generation began by criticizing and expanding Marx's concept of labor. Marx speaks of the dual character of labor, as it creates both exchange value and use value. Thus,

> Marx centered wage labor as the determining factor in shaping the activity of life. This argument had the effect that the male worker in his historical role as breadwinner of the family became the center of analysis, just as the labor movement became the subject of politics.
>
> HAUG, 2015: 309[5]

In the capitalist mode of production, which is characterized by the separation of factory and domestic work, the role of women and the production of life initially received little attention. However, the "production of food"

---

4 These include, for example, the socialists who were concerned with the so-called women's question at the turn of the century, such as August Bebel, Frederick Engels, Alexandra Kollontai, Johanna Löwenherz, Adelheid Popp, Clara Zetkin, and others.
5 We would like to thank Kerstin Wolter for the discussions on this contribution and the reference to various quotations from Frigga Haug.

(production) and the "production of life" (reproduction) are mutually constitutive (Ibid: 326). Frigga Haug identifies the origin of women's marginalized position in the superordination of the sphere of production over the sphere of reproduction (Haug, 2011). In this sense, she also speaks of gender relations as relations of production (Haug, 2015: 241, 325). This means that "the gender-specific division of social areas of work and their hierarchical arrangement [...] have resulted in the social oppression of women to this day (Die Linke Mecklemburg-Vorpommern, 2011)." From a similar perspective, Mariarosa Dalla Costa and Selma James, among others, had previously formulated the criticism that reproductive labor is also productive labor because it produces the commodity labor in the first place (James, 1972: 97). Silvia Federici traces the historical development of the privatization of reproduction with the advent of capitalism (Federici, 2004), whereby the area in which life is produced, nursed and maintained, and the people who carry out the majority of these tasks became marginalized in society. Feminists around Dalla Costa, James and Federici developed the demand for a wage for domestic work. Often misunderstood, the activists were not concerned with further commercializing domestic work or keeping women in domestic work through remuneration (Davis, 1981b: 222–24). On the contrary, as Federici writes in *Wages Against Housework*, the demand for remuneration was intended to emphasize that these activities are work, and indeed fundamental work for the capitalist system (Federici, 2012: 15–22). Naming something as work is the first step towards mobilizing for a different organization of such work.

In the debate about the origins of patriarchal oppression and the connection between exploitation and oppression in general, the approaches of US sociologist Lise Vogel are once again being used today. Originating in the early 1980s, but largely overlooked at the time, her work was only rediscovered decades later in global Marxist-feminist discussions. Vogel considers a central question of social reproduction theory whether

> sex, race, and class [are] parallel oppressions of an essentially similar kind? Does female oppression have its own theoretically specific character? What is the relationship of the fight against women's oppression to the struggle for national liberation and for socialism.
> VOGEL, 2013: 7

To approach these questions, social reproduction theory considers analytical categories such as labor, economy and household "as *processes* rather than things (Ibid: xxxvii)." This perspective enables "the possibility of a more genuinely *historical*-materialist reading of the social relations of power, one that identifies the conditions under which race, gender, sexuality, and class are (co)-reproduced, transformed and potentially revolutionized (Ibid)." The discussion of these relations and the various aspects of domestic work (naturalized as feminine) is therefore directly related to restrictions on rights of freedom and various structural gendered disadvantages that have repeatedly bound women to home and hearth in one particular form or another throughout the history of class societies.

Although many of these historical debates about the relationship between class and gender were based explicitly on the role of women, they did not challenge the very concept of woman as a gender category and gave little consideration to racist and colonial structures, it would be a fallacy to negate the significance of these debates. Not only was the particular exploitation and oppression of Black and Third World women discussed as early as the 1970s, first among the US Left and later internationally.[6] These debates made it possible to understand how the separation into the spheres of production and reproduction, into private and public spheres and into non-remunerated and remunerated work establishes a specific racialized and gender binary hierarchy with the respective bodies ascribed to them.[7] Only such a historical and socially embedded understanding of gender can prevent a category – such as woman–from being essentialized and treated as ahistorically rigid and homogeneous.[8]

---

6 Third World woman emerged as a decidedly political term expressing solidarity between immigrant and/or non-white women in the West with women in colonial and semi-colonial countries of the Global South. In this sense, in the 1970s, the term was a marker for common struggles as well as for the dependence of global capital on the labor of Black and Brown bodies worldwide (Taylor, 2017: 11–12).

7 Some theories of social reproduction point to the processual nature of gendering and sexualization. Thus, the socially determined division of labor (domestic vs. commercial, interior vs. exterior, etc.) was and is attributed to certain bodies and thereby naturalized and ideologically legitimized (as well as with the help of patriarchal religions and misogynistic, gender-binary and heterosexist laws). Cf. Bernes and Chan, 2013: 56–90; Lugones, 2007. The centrality of these binary divisions can also be seen in the violence with which traditional role models as well as bisexuality, heterosexuality and cis-normativity continue to be upheld. Jules Joanne Gleeson describes how theories of social reproduction also have the potential to advance trans-inclusive and queer feminist theorizing. Here, materialist analyses show how private households dominate the subjects they prepare for the working environment, down to the most intimate experiences and identifications. Cf. Gleeson, 2019.

8 As Francoise Vergès emphasizes, women are not a political class per se. It is a category that evolves over time and functions in a way that is historically and locally specific (Vergès, 2019: 23).

3 Social Reproduction and Racism

Many contemporary strategies to combat racism begin and end with the individual. At the same time, the necessity to combine struggles against sexism with struggles against racism is often repeated like a mantra. Both of these constitute the essence of liberal anti-racism in the present era, even within feminist circles. However, they fail to address the roots of the problem (Mies, 1990: 19–20).[9] The continued existence of colonial conditions, imperialist exploitation and wars and their reproduction in everyday social relations, often remain invisible behind references to discriminatory statements and individual privileges, or are even legitimized by them.[10] Theories of social reproduction make it possible to illuminate everyday life and thus to understand the structures of neglected social spheres that are shaped by racism. With the category of social reproduction, we focus on all relationships between the workplace and all other institutions and processes that determine and reproduce labor. The frequently concealed or naturalized (super-)exploitation is not only organized along patriarchal lines, but also permeated by structural forms of racism.[11] This becomes apparent as soon as we understand that the reproduction of labor and society also happens in and through border controls, camps for asylum seekers or remittances from immigrants to their countries of origin (Dimitrakaki et al, 2016: 31).

Several of these points are particularly distilled in nursing and care work. Historically, care and domestic work have been devalued and outsourced not only along gendered lines, but also along colonial and racialized lines. It is therefore crucial to highlight these diverse spheres of reproduction not only as central sites of continued colonial appropriation and violence, but especially as sites of anti-colonial resistance (Hall, 2016: 88, 90). To illustrate this argument more tangibly, we will apply social reproduction theory to demonstrate how super-exploitation and reification occur in two historical spheres.

---

9 Maria Mies noted as early as 1990: "But although most white feminists today admit that feminism cannot achieve its goals unless racism is eradicated, efforts to understand the relationship between sexism and racism usually remain stuck at an individual level, where the individual woman explores her own inner self to discover and punish the 'racist' within herself (Mies, 1990: 19–20).

10 The way in which feminism and the "liberation of women" have been used for the "war on terror" from 2001 and as legitimization for the Iraq war in 2003 is just one such expression thereof. Cf. Mohanty, 2003; Ware, 1997. During German colonialism, white bourgeois women and feminists shaped practices, politics and imaginations about racial hierarchies and gender roles. Cf. Wildenthal, 2001.

11 See the contribution by Bafta Sarbo in this volume, pp. 16–35.

Finally, we present an outlook that suggests how these analyses can lead us to more radical conclusions regarding the entanglement of class, gender and *race* today.

4 Racism and Reproduction Throughout History

In order to understand the nature of contemporary social relations, it is worth examining the role of so-called private structures of family and kinship relations. These emerge as the privileged sites of the hidden negotiation over property relations and the formation of certain (wage) workers. In everyday life, the private sphere is marked as an isolated and distinct zone outside of capitalist relations of exploitation, as a self-responsible and color-blind space (Eng, 2010: 11–12).[12] This obscures the ways in which Western family relations and the bourgeois private sphere could only come about through enslaved, colonial and/or (contractually) obligated labor, especially in the form of housework. It created the material conditions for the private and public spheres, reproduction and production, to be separated in the first place. For example, women who were enslaved by Europeans on the American and African continents were objectified as bodies for the reproduction of new commodities. Children born to enslaved mothers were automatically given the same status and thus became the additional property of the slave owners at minimal cost (Davis, 1981a: 2–15). Thus, legalized practices of super-exploitation permeated the most intimate relationships,[13] namely sexualized exploitation for the purpose of direct reproduction.[14] The colonial regime of reproduction was thus also based on constant sexualized violence in the form of systematic rape (Davis, 1981a). Racist classifications emerged in the European colonies in order to organize the reproduction of the working subject and the social order.[15] This racist colonial class structure continues to impact the composition of class

---

12   Eng refers to this as the racialization of intimacy.
13   In 1662, the Partus-sequitur-ventrem law was passed in colonial Virginia and other British colonies. It stipulated that children always inherit the legal status of their mother (Morgan, 2018: 1–17).
14   Hortense Spillers (1987: 65–81), for example, shows how family and kinship relations are produced and racially categorized from colonial enslavement to the present day in her essay "Mama's Baby, Papa's Maybe: An American Grammar Book."
15   In some cases, categories were created in order to create different family and thus class relations that could be measured on the basis of a person's racial origin or mixture. In Spanish-speaking Latin America, so-called race charts were established. Depending on the degree of mestizaje, or admixture, it was possible to move up in the colonial order.

structures in the Caribbean and the Spanish- and Portuguese-speaking parts of the Americas to this day.

In today's neoliberal narrative, the responsibility for class affiliation and poverty is shifted to the private sphere of the family and the individual. This simultaneously emphasizes and perpetuates the classifications of class, gender, sexuality or *race* that have been created, but continues to render invisible their historical and material foundations. However, from the perspective of social reproduction theory, it becomes evident that the inclusion of the household, family, kinship relations, feminized bodies and social reproduction as important sites of systematic oppression and exploitation also paves the way for the discovery of their potential for resistance. For instance, Angela Davis and Alys Eve Weinbaum describe the resistance of enslaved women, which has often been overlooked or marginalized in the analyses of many anti-colonial thinkers Davis, 1981a; Weinbaum, 2013). The resistance of enslaved women was of tremendous importance to the legal end of slavery. Colonized women were active participants, not passive observers, of anti-colonial rebellions (Boisvert, 2001; Bush, 1990; Girard, 2009).[16] This knowledge is still relevant today for the political organizing of struggles that extend beyond feminism and anti-racism, because a collective archive of knowledge about forms of resistance should nurture and guide movements. In contrast to the conventional narrative of colonized women portrayed as passive, whether Irish or enslaved Africans, their active role in facilitating or impeding social reproductive labor, among other things, reveals a different picture of the contradictions within the political economy of colonial and colonizing societies.

Manuela Bojadžijev demonstrates how in West Germany during the recruitment of so-called guest workers from the 1950s onwards, immigrant workers organized early struggles at the immediate sites of their exploitation (Bojadžijev, 2012). Moreover, resistance also emerged in the realm of reproduction. Bojadžijev delineates how the "starting point of many protests was resistance against the denial of privacy (Ibid: 199)." In 1962, for instance, Italian workers at VW in Wolfsburg went on strike to protest their deplorable housing situation. The camp, which housed approximately 400 people, was surrounded by wire mesh fencing. The work stoppage was triggered by the death of a sick worker due to miserable medical care in the camp (Ibid: 200). The various rent strikes in Frankfurt am Main from 1970 onwards drew on the experiences of the Italian rent strike movement: Immigrant families joined forces with German neighbors and supporters to gain satisfactory long-term

---

16 See for examples from the Caribbean.

housing conditions for themselves and their families by ways of squatting, for example, but also to combat racism and the stigmatization by the press (Ibid: 205–10). From the mid-1970s onwards, the issues of school education and child benefits were taken up by immigrant workers and trade unions such as IG Metall (Ibid: 208–24; Goeke, 2020: 226–27). The institutionalized discrimination against the children of guest workers was subjected to sharp criticism and opposition, as were the cuts to child benefits for this group. The SPD-FDP government enacted a new regulation on January 1, 1975, which provided for an increase in child benefits for Germans and a select group of immigrant workers, including those who had been employed in the FRG for over 15 years (Bojadžijev, 2012: 218). In opposition to this, child benefit committees were established in 19 cities, "which coordinated nationwide, campaigned against the discrimination of immigrants and – beyond the issue of child benefit – demanded equal rights for Germans and foreigners (Ibid: 219)." Even though the collective memories of these struggles in the field of reproduction live on in poems, song lyrics, novels and autobiographies (Ibid: 198), they have often been suppressed in proletarian and anti-racist historiography. The concept of social reproduction theory therefore allows us to understand struggles for rent, education and social benefits as part of anti-racist class struggles in the history of the labor movement in Germany.

5 Global Reproduction Today

Patriarchal and racist structures permeate all social relations. They are modified and sometimes exacerbated by new or newly created global organizational structures. Today, processes of migration play a central role in regimes of reproduction (Ferguson and McNally, 2015). From the perspective of social reproduction theory, the increased precarization of immigrant workers is a deliberate policy and not collateral damage. For example, the permanent threat of deportation faced by undocumented immigrants and the terror associated with it intensifies racialized forms of precarity and maintains people in a state of control and dependence (Ibid: 6). Today's hyper-precarious migration policy functions as a means of appropriating the labor of dispossessed people from the periphery and must therefore be understood as a particularly crucial aspect of capitalist reproduction and population policy.

The increase in global proletarianization and precarization is thus a means to an end: the capitalist mode of production is dependent on gendered and racialized relations that enable the constant supply of this and subsequent generations of cheap labor. Particularly since the onset of neoliberalization in the 1970s, migration programs have increasingly linked employment, residency rights and citizenship, introducing legal forms of discrimination that inscribe precarious work with precarious residency status into the foundations of liberal democracies (Hopkins, 2017: 137; Ha, 2007: 31–71). This is particularly evident in the increasing migration from the Global South to the Global North for paid domestic, sex, care and nursing work (Farris, 2012; Farris, 2017). These movements disguise the dependence of the countries of arrival on this work, while new dependencies on remittances arise in the countries of origin. This restructures communities and economic systems in the sending countries and opens them up to neoliberal takeovers. Transnational social reproduction is therefore also a key factor in understanding the increasing precarity of countries on the periphery or in the Global South (Hopkins, 2017: 137). The fact that paid domestic work is structured according to racialized and racist patterns is not a novel one. Long before wages were demanded for domestic work, poor, and often racially marginalized women were working for low pay in rich people's homes. Racism and sexism facilitate exploitation, violence and abuse. This phenomenon also occurs through the positive attribution of characteristics. The essentialist argument that women are naturally suited for care work is reflected in numerous everyday discussions and economic programs. Sara R. Farris therefore refers to immigrant female labor as a "regular army" (instead of a reserve army) of available labor. This is because migration policy has never been formulated in a gender-neutral way. Farris describes how "the image of the immigrant as male *Gastarbeiter* (guest worker) that was diffused in the 1950s and 1960s, when Europe received the first significant flows of foreigners from all over the world, has now been replaced by the figure of the migrant as a female maid (Farris, 2012: 184)." Farris uses the term *femonationalism* to describe the discourse and the neoliberal state and non-state integration programs that bring together heterogeneous anti-migration debates under the invocation of discussions around gender justice (Ibid: 187). Central feminist battlegrounds such as protection against sexualized violence are thus exploited for racist campaigns.[17] In the process, female immigrants are explicitly positioned as feminine objects in need of rescue, while male immigrants are positioned as patriarchal threats.[18]

---

17   This has a long tradition. For example, the brutal lynchings in the American South at the turn of the century were carried out in the name of protecting white women, as Ida B. Wells pointed out in *Lynching, Our National Crime* (Address at the National Negro Conference, New York, 1909.) The debates surrounding and following New Year's Eve 2015 in Cologne are exemplary of a current revival of these dynamics.

18   Similar discussions can also be found in narratives surrounding sexuality. For example, norms such as liberal openness towards (homo)sexuality are used as exclusionary tactics

At the same time, immigrants are indispensable for the economies of capitalist centers such as Germany, although the treatment of workers in these centers varies significantly along gender lines. Despite the economic crisis of 2008, paid reproductive labor, especially care and domestic work, has been among the constantly increasing sectors since 2002 (Farris, 2012: 190). The increased entry of immigrant women into this sector is the main reason for the feminization of migration. It is only because of the work of immigrants that women in Europe who are better off are able to experience a certain liberation from care and domestic work and make greater use of their labor in production (Ibid: 193).

Female immigrant workers and their daughters thus serve (a) as cheap labor in those sectors where native women (white, Western European and protected by residence law) are no longer willing to work, and at the same time (b) as a canvas for ideological projections in the public debate on headscarf bans, intimate partner violence, sexualized violence and even femicide. This reinforces both the patriarchal sexual contract that assigns care and domestic work to women and a racist contract according to which ethnic minorities and non-white people are expected to perform the least valued and recognized tasks in society (Ibid: 194).

6   Class, Gender and *Race*: An Outlook

An effective analysis and policy that goes beyond liberal-individualist rhetoric and empty universal-cosmopolitan lip service requires an understanding of the different ways in which people are classified. Processes of gender assignment and racialization do not function in the same way. In the course of the capitalist mode of production's formation, the division of labor based on physical-reproductive functions has assigned some bodies with specific generalized characteristics to one sector of production. Although gender and *race* do not function in the same way and gender appeared historically as a structural category centuries before *race*, they are often mobilized – and often intertwined – by using naturalizing arguments to assign people to specific areas of (re)production and then legitimizing it through ideology.

---

for immigration policy in many countries. This specific discursive framework was highlighted by Jasbir Puar in her critique of homonationalism. Here, she criticizes how certain LGBTQI + narratives have produced discourses of modernity and progress that exclude certain populations from citizenship and society in general (Puar, 2017).

A framework based on Marxist-feminist reproduction theory allows us to grasp the specific entanglement of class, gender and *race* more concretely. Furthermore, it becomes evident that struggles for human liberation cannot be exclusively feminist, anti-patriarchal or anti-racist. In order to achieve a socialist mobilization in all areas and spaces between them, it is essential to comprehend all ascribed categories, including gender, *race*, sexuality, and so forth. These categories must be understood in their significance for the capitalist economic system and criticized accordingly, both in theory and in practice.

Bibliography

Arruzza, Cinzia (2017) *Feminismus und Marxismus. Eine Einführung*. Köln: Neuer isp Verlag.

Bhattacharya, Tithi (2017) *Social Reproduction Theory: Remapping Class, Recentering Oppression*. London: Pluto Press.

Bernes, Jasper and Chris Chan (2013) The Logic of Gender: On the Separation of Spheres and the Process of Abjection. In: *Endnotes 3: Gender, Race, Class and Other Misfortunes*. Berkeley: Little Black Cart.

Bojadžijev, Manuela (2012) *Die windige Internationale. Rassismus und Kämpfe der Migration*. Münster: Dampfboot Verlag.

Burns, Rebecca (2019) What's at Stake in Chicago Teachers' Strike: Whether Unions Can Bargain for the Entire Working Class, *In These Times*, October 14, inthesetimes.com/working/entry/22115/chicago-teachers-union-strike-ctu-lightfoot-seiu-housing-labor.

Davis, Angela (1981a) Reflections on the Black Woman's Role in the Community of Slaves, *The Black Scholar*, vol. 12, no. 6, jstor.org/stable/41066850.

Davis, Angela (1981b) *Women, Race and Class*. London: Women's Press, 1981.

Die Linke Mecklenburg-Vorpommern (2011) Geschlechterverhältnisse sind Produktionsverhältnisse, *Originalsozial*, originalsozial.de/politik/programm/ii-krisen-des-kapitalismus-krisen-der-zivilisation/geschlechterverhaeltnisse-sind-produktionsverhaeltnisse.

Dimitrakaki, Angela et al. (2016) Introduction, *Historical Materialism. Special Issue on Social Reproduction*, vol. 24, no. 2, DOI: 10.1163/1569206X-12341469.

Eng, David (2010) *The Feeling of Kinship. Queer Liberalism and the Racialization of Intimacy*. Durham: Duke University Press.

Farris, Sara R. (2012) Femonationalism and the 'Regular' Army of Labor Called Migrant Women, *History of the Present*, vol. 2, no. 2, pp. 184–199, jstor.org/stable/10.5406/historypresent.2.2.0184.

Farris, Sara R. (2017) *In the Name of Women's Rights. The Rise of Femonationalism.* Durham/London: Duke University Press.

Federici, Silvia (2004) *Caliban and the Witch. Women, The Body and Primitive Accumulation.* New York: Autonomedia.

Federici, Silvia (2012) *Revolution at Point Zero: Housework, Reproduction, and Feminist Struggle.* New York: PM Press.

Ferguson, Susan and David McNally (2015) Precarious Migrants: Gender, Race, and the Social Reproduction of a Global Working Class, *Socialist Register*, vol. 51, pp. 1–23, socialistregister.com/index.php/srv/issue/view/1578.

Gleeson, Jules Joanne (2019) An Aviary of Queer Social Reproduction, *Hypocrite Reader*, vol. 94, hypocritereader.com/94/eggs-queer-social-reproduction.

Goeke, Simon (2020) *"Wir sind alle Fremdarbeiter!" Gewerkschaften, migrantische Kämpfe und soziale Bewegungen in Westdeutschland 1960–1980.* Paderborn: Brill | Schöningh.

Ha, Kien Nghi (2007) Koloniale Arbeitsmigrationspolitik im Imperial Germany. In: Nicola Lauré al-Samarai et al. (eds.), *re/visionen. Postkoloniale Perspektiven von People of Color auf Rassismus, Kulturpolitik und Widerstand in Deutschland* Münster: unrast Verlag.

Hall, Rebecca (2016) Reproduction and Resistance: An Anti-colonial Contribution to Social Reproduction Theory, *Historical Materialism*, vol. 24, no. 2, DOI: 10.1163/1569206X-12341473.

Hartmann, Heidi (1981) The Unhappy Marriage of Marxism and Feminism. In: Lydia Sargent (ed.), *Women and Revolution.* Montréal: Black Rose Books Ltd.

Haug, Frigga (2015) *Der im Gehen erkundete Weg. Marxismus-Feminismus.* Hamburg: Argument Verlag.

Haug, Frigga (2011) *Die Vier-in-einem-Perspektive: Politik von Frauen für eine neue Linke.* Hamburg: Argument Verlag.

Hopkins, Carmen Teeple (2017) Mostly Work, Little Play: Social Reproduction, Migration, and Paid Domestic Work in Montreal. In: Tithi Bhattacharya (2017) *Social Reproduction Theory: Remapping Class, Recentering Oppression.* London: Pluto Press.

Jaffe, Aaron (2020) *Social Reproduction Theory and the Socialist Horizon.* London: Pluto Press.

James, Selma (1972) The Power of Women and the Subversion of the Community (1972) [Excerpts]. In: Selma James (2012) *Sex, Race and Class. The Perspective of Winning. A Selection of Writings 1952–2011.* Oakland: PM Press.

Lugones, María (2007) Heterosexualism and the Colonial/Modern Gender System, *Hypatia, Inc.*, vol. 22, no. 1, pp. 186–209, jstor.org/stable/4640051.

Mies, Maria (1990) *Patriarchat und Kapital. Frauen in der internationalen Arbeitsteilung.* Zürich: bge-Verlag.

Mohanty, Chandra Talpade (2003) *Feminism Without Borders. Decolonizing Theory, Practicing Solidarity*. Durham and London: Duke University Press.

Morgan, Jennifer L. (2018) Partus Sequitur Ventrem: Law, Race, and Reproduction in Colonial Slavery, *Small Axe*, vol. 22, no. 1, muse.jhu.edu/article/689365.

Ni Una Menos (2018) Call to the International Women's Strike – March 8, 2018, *Critical Times*, vol. 1, no. 1, pp. 268–69, DOI: 10.1215/26410478-1.1.268.

Puar, Jasbir (2017) *Terrorist Assemblages: Homonationalism in Queer Times*. Durham: Duke University Press.

Spillers, Hortense (1987) Mama's Baby, Papa's Maybe: An American Grammar Book," *Diacritics*, vol. 17, no. 2, DOI: 10.2307/464747.

Taylor, Keeanga-Yamahtta (2017) *How We Get Free. Black Feminism and the Combahee River Collective*. Chicago: Haymarket Books.

Vergès, Francoise (2019) *A Decolonial Feminism*. London: Pluto Press.

Vogel, Lise (2013) *Marxism and the Oppression of Women*. Leiden and Boston: Brill.

Ware, Vron (1997) *Beyond the Pale: White Women, Racism and History*. London: Verso.

Weinbaum, Alys Eve (2013) Gendering the General Strike: W.E.B. Du Bois's Black Reconstruction and Black Feminism's 'Propaganda of History,' *The South Atlantic Quarterly*, vol. 112, no. 3, pp. 437–63, DOI: 10.1215/00382876-2146395.

Wildenthal, Lora (2001) *German Women for Empire, 1884–1945*. Durham: Duke University Press.

CHAPTER 4

Racism in the European Migration and Border Regime from the Perspective of a Materialist Theory of Domination

Fabian Georgi

Since the early 2010s, right-wing political forces and the milieus of an increasingly authoritarian center have been justifying their demands for stricter migration and asylum policies in Germany in an explicitly racist manner, more openly, more loudly and more visibly than in previous years (Decker and Brähler, 2020). Prepared in part by the anti-Muslim discourse after 9/11 and Thilo Sarrazin's 2010 book *Deutschland Schafft Sich Ab* (Germany abolishes itself), since 2014 one of the most important right-wing networks of the last decade has been formulating its cultural racist program of border isolation, already contained in its name: Patriotische Europäer gegen die Islamisierung des Abendlands (Patriotic Europeans against the Islamization of the West).

This chapter addresses the question of how the latest surge in racism shapes migration, asylum, and border policies in Germany and the EU. It also considers the converse question of how the complex struggles of the European migration and border regime influence the dynamics of racism in Germany. Based on these questions and the aim of this volume to further develop Marxist analyses of racism, this chapter has two objectives.[1] First, I outline – as a thesis and an offer to debate – a concept of racism that understands it as a relation of re/production that is formed or structured by domination. This understanding suggests that racism "solves" problems of material and social reproduction through domination, which privileges and favors the satisfaction of the needs of certain groups. Second, I examine the extent to which this conceptualization of racism can be productive for investigating conjunctures of racism. This examination will focus on the intertwined dynamics of racism and the European migration and border regime.

Along four theses, I argue that racist forces in Germany have suffered social and political defeats in recent decades. However, the irregular practices of

---

1 I would like to thank Lars Bretthauer, Sonja Buckel, Dirk Martin, Anna Steenblock, Sacha Radl and the editors for helpful comments and criticism on arguments or excerpts from this chapter.

flight and migration employed by members of the global working class to reach Germany, in the context of the profound structural and multifaceted crises of the capitalist world system, presented opportunities for racist forces to mobilize in opposition. This was also successful because racism continued to be advantageous for a significant proportion of the German population, enabling the legitimization of practices of domination such as exploitation and exclusion, devaluation and control.

1   Racism from the Perspective of a Historical Materialist Theory of Domination

1.1   *Relations of Domination as Relations of Re/production*

Many critical race scholars argue that racism should not be understood solely as a pattern of prejudice or attitude, nor primarily as a way of thinking, ideology or discourse. Instead, they interpret racism as a specific relation of domination between people (Roldán Mendívil and Sarbo, 2021). "Racism," according to Étienne Balibar (1988: 41), is "a social relation, not the mere ravings of racist subjects." This understanding of racism raises the question of what is actually meant by the term "relation of domination." Although the term is used excessively today, it remains largely undefined in the context of social theory. For what purposes do people exercise domination and enter into relations of domination? How are relations of domination connected to the relations of material re/production, which are central to Marxist theorization? In order to sharpen a critical understanding of racism, I will outline elements of a historical-materialist concept of domination.

In the *Historical-Critical Dictionary of Marxism*, Werner Goldschmidt (2004: 83) defines domination "not [as] an isolated action or chain of actions, but an institutionalized, structurally asymmetrical power relation of superiority or subordination between social units (individuals, groups or classes, etc.)." Domination should not be "reduced to economic terms," for example to the "institutionalized appropriation of other people's labor […] without compensation (Ibid: 83–84)." Instead, the "appropriation [through domination] of all possible objects of human needs and desires, that is, the totality of all possible interests, must be included (Ibid: 84)." Wolf-Dieter Narr (2012: 42; 2015: 89–91) also emphasizes the complexity of human driving forces (he mentions, among other things, "hunger, sexuality, forms of social recognition, self-determination, thought and action"), which can drive attempts by powerful groups to establish, defend and modify power relations in order to prioritize their own complex and historically contingent needs.

However, in order to ensure the long-term satisfaction of these privileged needs and to overcome the constant emergence of new problems and resistance, power relations are not solely based on the practices of *exploitation* and *appropriation* mentioned by Goldschmidt[2] (Spehr, 2003: 35). In my view, it is beneficial to distinguish at least three additional forms of practice carried out within relations of domination that aim to "create the kind of world the ruler dreams of (Ibid)." These intertwined practices include the symbolic-discursive devaluation of oppressed groups for psychological purposes, the hierarchized exclusion from social surplus and the tendency to violently control potential disruptions to domination.

Now, from a materialist perspective, it is crucial that these forms of practice and the privileged satisfaction of needs which they enable are exercised centrally with regard to the organization of work within society, that is, to the social relations of production within which this work is performed and in which its products are distributed and appropriated. Sonja Buckel notes that "work within society and the control over it are decisive for the complex context of domination (Buckel, 2015: 33)." This refers to the basic idea of historical materialism. It consists of the fact that the dynamics of human societies are shaped and driven by those historically specific relations in which people to a large degree are forced to materially and practically re/produce themselves, their families, households and communities through work and in relation to other people as well as through the metabolism between humans and nature, that is, to sustain their own lives and social existence in relations of re/production based on the division of labor (Marx, 1987: 41–45). In order to survive and to fulfill complex, contingent needs, people must constantly solve the challenges and problems of the material re/production of their material provisions, their reproduction and their sociality. This is "a fundamental condition of all history, which, [...] must daily and hourly be fulfilled [...] (Ibid: 42)."

This is the primary rationale behind the prioritization of the relations of production and reproduction in materialist theories. These theories analyze and interpret specific individuals, groups, or institutions (as well as specific racist practices, discourses and policies) within the context of these relations and analyze how these relations shape and reshape these entities. The historically

---

2 Christoph Spehr has presented a different concept of domination that focuses on appropriation processes: "Domination is forced social cooperation. Cooperation is enforced because one side cannot free itself from it, because it cannot determine what it contributes and under what conditions, because it has little or no influence on the rules of cooperation." Christoph Spehr, *Gleicher als andere: Eine Grundlegung der freien Kooperation* (Berlin: Karl Dietz Verlag, 2003), 35.

specific conditions of the material re-/production of human life and the practices, contradictions and struggles associated with them significantly influence the forms, dynamics and potentials of human societies, including those of racism. This is because the problems and challenges of sustaining human life are all-encompassing, large and permanent. This is because the problems of the fulfillment of human life needs is so difficult and complex to realize that the struggles waged over these problems, the practices pursued with these goals and the resulting contradictions constitute and shape the forms and dynamics of human societies, including those of racism, to a considerable degree (Brenkert, 2010: 45–50).

1.2 Relations of Domination in the Capitalist Mode of Re/production

In order to gain a materialist understanding of racism, it is now crucial to recognize that the relations of domination that people have established historically and in the present for the purpose of privileged satisfaction of needs are complex and intertwined (Buckel, 2015: 31). Especially in societies "in which the capitalist mode of production prevails (Marx, 1996: 45)," the social relations within which the people of a given period organize their material and social re/production for the benefit of dominant and privileged social groups do not consist solely of class relations resulting from the position of groups in the sphere of production. Materialist feminists have demonstrated that gender relations in the form of domination have always been an integral part of capitalist modes of re/production. Without patriarchal and sexist relations of re/production, the appropriation of free reproductive labor in families and the super-exploitation of female wage labor in care sectors, which are a prerequisite for capital relations and profit production, would not be possible (Bhattacharya, 2017: 1–20).

Similarly, Marxist theorists of racism have demonstrated on numerous occasions that stable and expanding capital accumulation has been dependent on constructing, deepening, politicizing and using external and internal differences between people in order to disenfranchise, divide and pit dominated groups against each other, primarily with the aim of justifying and enforcing their (super)exploitation, devaluation, exclusion and control (Roldán Mendivil and Sarbo, 2021: 299–300; Rodney, 2018: 102–04). Without the racially legitimized conquests, expropriations and exploitations that occurred during colonialism and continue to this day, the so-called original accumulation would not have been possible, nor would the surplus profits of today's industries, such as agriculture, construction, nursing or delivery services. These industries realize their profits mainly through the super-exploitation of labor that is racially discriminated against and/or disenfranchised by migration policy. Racist relations have been an integral part of capitalist modes of re/production. The term capitalism, therefore, encompasses an entire "mode of socialization (Buckel, 2015: 32)" that is constituted by several relations of domination, including the system of "sovereign (nation) states" and capitalist relations between nature and society. "The historical particularity of capitalism is precisely to interweave all these relations into a complex whole (Ibid)."

However, the diversity of relations of re/production that are structured by domination and their practical forms, historical articulations and constellations should not be imagined as if they were primarily enforced "from above," as if the functional interaction of class relations, sexism, racism, domination of nature and state power were designed, coordinated and enforced by a ruling clique in order to maintain the capitalist modes of re/production "as such." Although the strategic actions of ruling groups are highly relevant to the understanding of historical dynamics, capitalism as a whole, lacks a conscious, controlling, or coordinating center. Instead, the relations of re/production that are structured by domination and their institutionalization emerge and reproduce themselves primarily as the result of concrete strategies and social struggles with which different social groups, which are also intersectionally divided and hierarchized within themselves, attempt in very specific historical situations to shape re/production to their own advantage and/or to assert their privileged satisfaction of needs against obstacles and resistance. As relations of domination do not constitute a functional uniform system, but rather arise from the strategic practices of certain groups and are reproduced, modified and defended by them, different relations of domination and their historical articulations can develop dynamically and inconsistently and come into conflict with each other.

1.3 *Racism as a Relation of Re/production That is Structured by Domination*

From the perspective of the concept of domination outlined here, racism also presents itself as a material relation of re/production and the result of historically specific strategies employed by certain social groups to satisfy material, social and/or psychological needs in a privileged manner. This is achieved by establishing racist relations of re/production or (re)organizing or modifying the relations of re/production in society as a whole according to racist logics. These strategies involve the exploitation, devaluation, exclusion and/or control of groups racialized as inferior.[3] David Camfield (2016: 47) posits that

---

3 See also the article by Bafta Sarbo in this volume, pp. 16–35.

membership in racially oppressed groups is determined by ethnicized differences that are treated as inherited or de facto immutable, such as skin and hair color and/or cultural characteristics. Camfield further asserts that racially oppressed groups are multi-gendered and are not targeted on the basis of sexual orientation or perceived disabilities. This is how racism can be distinguished from sexism, heteronormativity and ableism (Ibid).

When racism is understood in this way, it becomes clear that, from a materialist perspective, the term also includes racist discourses, ways of thinking, language patterns or ideologies, but that these are interpreted as partial elements of a relation of re/production that is structured by domination. From a materialist perspective, the pervasive and influential racist discourses and ways of speaking arise and are maintained primarily because they assist racially privileged groups in legitimizing and enforcing specific practices and effects of their domination, in solving specific problems of domination and in regulating specific consequences (Ibid: 43–45, 57; Bonilla-Silva, 2014: 9).

However, the material advantages that privileged groups derive from racist relations of domination must not be understood in purely material-physical terms. For a further development of Marxist analyses of racism, it seems productive to me, as indicated above, to take the diversity of human "needs or desires, that is, the totality of all possible interests (Goldschmidt, 2004: 84)" as a starting point in order to distinguish practices and functions of racism more precisely. Racist relations of domination can thus, among other things, contribute to:

- enabling and legitimizing the (*super*)*exploitation* of the labor, resources and emotions of certain groups, whether in the form of "free wage labor" or through elements of coercion, plunder and robbery (today, for example, the exploitation of African harvest workers in southern Italy is reminiscent of slavery);
- justifying the *exclusion* or subordinate positioning of certain groups in the distribution of social surplus, for example in terms of income, housing conditions, health or education (today, for example, access to social benefits is dependent on residence status);
- legitimizing the social and symbolic *devaluation* of groups racialized as inferior, whereby dominant groups receive social and psychological advantages, such as recognition, a sense of superiority or an explanation of the world (today, for example, conspiracy theories of anti-Muslim racism);
- exercising or legitimizing *control* over the actions or development opportunities of racialized groups and thus preventing these groups from effectively defending themselves against their dominated position, evading it

or disrupting prevailing conditions (for example, police repression against protests in collective accommodation for refugees).

The functions of domination and thus the practices of domination that are historically relevant and effective in each constellation depend on a variety of conditions, including productive forces and relations of re/production, power relations and social struggles. In light of these dynamic factors, the form, functions and strategies of racism shift in the course of historical development. Consequently, there is no such thing as pure racism; rather, there are only historically specific forms of racisms (Hall, 1980: 335) that fulfill specific functions of domination in certain historical contexts. "Racism," according to Manuela Bojadžijev (2006), "is not a fixed ideological pattern, but its character is subject to change: its arguments, its objects, its appearance, its goals, its forms of organization. In this respect, we can only examine the surges in racism throughout history."

One of the challenges in analyzing the intertwined surges in racism and the European migration and border regime is to understand how the dynamics of racism can be analyzed and explained as the result of specific social struggles (Bonilla-Silva, 2001: 45). The struggles of those groups that are negatively affected by racism and that are directly and indirectly opposed to the causes, forms and effects of racist relations of domination must be understood as key dynamics here, because they constantly force racism to adapt (Balibar and Wallerstein, 1988: 54). At the same time, the struggles surrounding racism and migration and asylum policy should be decoded as complex and multifaceted social (class) conflicts in which numerous transnationally located social forces are involved. With regard to racism in Germany, these include movements of refugees and immigrant workers, *communities of color* (i.e. groups affected by racism and their informal and formal networks), liberal institutions and left-wing activists, trade unions and charities that often act ambivalently, various factions of capital as well as organized nationalist and racist forces. In order to understand the current role of racism in the European migration and border regime, it is therefore necessary to analyze the struggles between these and other forces.[4] The following section presents a summary of the results of such an analysis in the form of four theses.[5]

---

4   Following Antonio Gramsci and Nicos Poulantzas, among others, I have summarized suggestions on how such investigations can be implemented in the approach of a materialist migration and border regime analysis (Georgi, 2022: 384–402).
5   An earlier form of the argument developed here can be found in Georgi, 2019b: 102–110.

2 Flight, Migration and Racism in the European Border Regime

2.1 *Thesis 1: Backlash against Defeats Enabled Racist Mobilizations*

The rise of racist forces in Germany, their greater visibility and aggression in recent years were initially a backlash against defeats that they had suffered as a result of refugee and migration movements as well as anti-racist struggles. These defeats unsettled and outraged milieus susceptible to the right, which organized right-wing forces used for mobilization, election campaigns and racist violence and which materialized in a significantly more restrictive asylum and migration policy. Two defeats can be distinguished.

Firstly, anti-racist forces, immigrant networks and communities of color have fought for tangible achievements. Compared to the 1980s, there are more people living in Germany whose families often have complex migration histories and whose presence is often a thorn in the side of racist forces. According to official statistics, the proportion of people "with a migration background" in Germany rose from just over 18% to almost 26% between 2005 and 2019 alone (Statistisches Bundesamt, 2020: 66). This development has been accepted or even supported by a wider political spectrum and broader social milieus, which is reflected in the fact that people of color are now more visible in higher social positions, such as in media, culture, politics, sports and business. Overt, traditional forms of racism have been, to some extent, countered: "(Former) immigrants and their descendants are demanding equal participation to a greater extent and more successfully than ever and are pushing for new ways to repudiate and legally combat discrimination and racist exclusion (Espahangizi et. al., 2016: 14–15)." Racist forces that imagine Germany as a purely white society and/or who advocate racial stratification of social participation of people in Germany have seen all of these processes as defeats. The summer of migration in 2015/16, when over a million people found protection and life opportunities in Germany, was also a catastrophic setback from the perspective of these forces.[6]

Secondly, a "progressive neoliberalism (Fraser, 2017)" has developed since the 1990s, whose migration policies were an affront to racist forces. While the policy of European migration management was largely driven by an implicit coalition of right-wing conservative and neoliberal forces until the end of the 1990s, the balance of power behind this policy shifted at least gradually to the disadvantage of right-wing and racist forces from the early 2000s onwards.

---

6 For a materialist analysis of the summer of migration, its background and consequences, see in detail Georgi, 2019a: 205–27.

From the turn of the millennium, neoliberal actors increasingly attempted to achieve their goal of "regulated openness" for desired labor migration no longer primarily by pushing for isolation against unwanted migration using martial rhetoric. Instead, they increasingly tried to convince skeptical parts of the electorate with a rhetoric of diversity and multiculturalism and emphasized the economic benefits of migration (Georgi, 2019b: 104–06). Notwithstanding the fact that neoliberal experts and business associations have consistently supported the repressive implementation of migration policy and have emphasized the necessity for repressive EU "external border protection" with greater fervor since 2016, under pressure from the right-wing (Hoffmann, 2021: 99), racist forces have had to perceive as a threat the positive attitude towards migration and in some cases towards refugees, which was articulated during the summer of migration and can be understood as part of a "progressive neoliberalism." The achievements of the relational autonomy of migration and anti-racist struggles, as well as their partial integration and consolidation in progressive-neoliberal milieus and elite strategies, have at least partially weakened racist forces in Germany. Their resurgence is a counter-reaction to these anti-racist successes.

Nevertheless, such defeats for racist forces do not explain why their counter-mobilizations found such strong support since the 2010s. In light of the understanding of racism as a relation of re/production in the form of domination as outlined above, it can be argued that the racist backlash was partially successful because racism continues to perform important functions for large sections of the German population and solves problems of domination.

2.2 Thesis 2: Racism Fulfills Psychological Functions in "Damaged Life" (Adorno, 2018) under Capitalism

Firstly, the recent surge in racism could be interpreted as a result of the psychological functions it still fulfills for many individuals and groups today. Based on the concept of the "authoritarian personality (Adorno, 2019)," critical racism research today also concludes that the discursive and symbolic devaluation of certain groups through anti-egalitarian and chauvinistic resentments can help racially privileged individuals to psychologically process and channel experiences of frustration, powerlessness, insecurity and aggression. According to Adorno's classic interpretation, many people who reside in societies that organize their material re/production in a capitalist manner frequently suffer from an "ego weakness" which arises from the denial of fulfilling basic needs and emotional desires as well as from the inability to substantially influence the conditions of their own lives (Adorno, 2000: 57). Klaus Dörre et al. succinctly describe the resulting ethnicization of the social question:

> Because it appears hopeless to fundamentally correct relations of distribution perceived as unjust, wage earners spontaneously tend to redefine disputes between top and bottom as conflicts between internal and external. The tendency towards exclusive solidarity is taken up and reinforced by organized right-wing populism.
>
> DÖRRE ET AL., 2018

Following Ulrike Marz, it can be argued that in the face of the disappointments and existential insecurity inherent to capitalist life, which has been further exacerbated by the capitalist structural and multiple crises since 2008 and their authoritarian-neoliberal treatment, at least part of the German population is attempting to compensate for this "permanent narcissistic grievance (Marz, 2017: 255)" through a collective narcissism directed against minority groups.

> As a conformist revolt, racist subjects direct aggression, psychological strain and powerlessness that are typical products of modern subject formation at people and racialized groups perceived as foreign or non-German, instead of directing them against abstract domination.
>
> Ibid: 250

According to such interpretations, racism allows racist subjects to feel superior as they look down on devalued racial groups. Furthermore, racism can provide them with psychological benefits such as explanation of the world and scapegoating: When the real reasons for narcissistic slights, frustrated hopes, instinctual frustrations, and damaged lives lie beyond comprehension or the power to change them, arguably it can be psychologically "rational" to project the resulting resentments onto inferior groups. These psychological functions of racism may be even more important than ever in the 2010s for many people, such as those in the AfD's milieus and social bases.

2.3   Thesis 3: Racism Legitimizes Exclusion from Surplus Distribution

Another reason why racism persists and grows in Europe is that it serves to legitimate exclusion, graduated disenfranchisement, and differential inclusion of non-citizens through border regimes and migration policies for racially privileged groups in Germany and the EU. From a Marxist perspective, the exclusion of non-citizens from the territory of the EU or the hierarchized access to social and political rights and public services based on their residence status can be understood as a graduated exclusion from the enjoyment of social surplus. This exclusion can be conceptualized as a low, subordinate hierarchization in the sphere of distribution. Racist discourses and ideologies which justify the existence and necessity of restrictive border regimes for many people also have the advantage of legitimizing the ability of these people to treat others as subordinate or to completely exclude them from the distribution of the social surplus. Conversely, these people are able to enjoy material advantages themselves (Camfield, 2016: 54–55; Bonilla-Silva, 2014: 9).

The necessity to justify and legitimize migration and border policy exclusion and disenfranchisement to oneself, the public, and the world at large can appear all the more urgent in the current historical situation. This is because the material, social, and psychological benefits experienced by many people as citizens of the Global North, i.e. as beneficiaries of an imperial mode of living and of production (Brand and Wissen, 2017) or a "reproduction mechanism of capitalist socialization" that "externalizes" its costs outwards and downwards (Lessenich, 2018: 23) are fundamentally dependent on migration and border policy exclusion. The starkly disparate relations of re/production and modes of living in the Global North and South could not have a stable existence without the violent border regimes that separate them (Georgi, 2019c). In the context of economic and social crises, many EU citizens perceive refugees and immigrants from regions of the world that have been impoverished by imperialism as a source of increased competition and a threat to their material advantages. The racially motivated protection of advantages resulting from a privileged position in North-South relations through restrictive border regimes thus has a perfidious, self-serving rationale. The restrictive shift in German and European migration and border policy since 2015 can also be explained by the greater influence of racist forces and their more successful mobilization of racist resentments.

2.4   Thesis 4: Racism Enables Super-Exploitation and Division of Workers

Another problem of domination that racism helps to solve in Germany and the EU is that it facilitates exploitation on the labor market of those who are racially subordinated and disenfranchised in terms of citizenship, residence status and in sociopolitical terms by companies and shareholders. Moreover, it enables the imposition of lower wages and inferior working conditions.[7] Racism enables this, among other things, because wage earners who are racially discriminated against often lack access to jobs with better conditions, given that their residence status prevents them from changing employers or because they need jobs subject to social security contributions in order to consolidate their residence status. For companies, racist discrimination and migration

---

7   See the contribution by Bafta Sarbo in this volume, pp. 16–35.

policy disenfranchisement thus contribute to solving the problem of remaining profitable in capitalist competition and generating extra profits (Roldán Mendívil and Sarbo, 2021: 301–02). Currently, racism continues to function as a "magic formula" (Balibar and Wallerstein, 1988: 33) that allows capitalists to exploit (immigrant) wage earners and their descendants more heavily while weakening the resistance of white labor by disenfranchising their co-workers who are racialized as non-white.

It is crucial to note that the possibility of exploiting racist hierarchizations for (super)exploitation is usually not justified or defended by "overtly" racist arguments. In contrast, shareholders and relevant sections of racially privileged groups actively resist migration, labor and social policy measures as well as radical democratic reforms that would actually push back against such super-exploitation enabled by racism (Camfield, 2016: 61). These measures include secure residency rights, equal and strong social and political rights for non-citizens, comprehensive anti-racist labor law reforms, strong trade union rights, and far-reaching anti-discrimination laws that could actually be enforced by well-funded institutions. By rejecting such initiatives from social movements and left-wing parties as expensive, inefficient or "unnecessarily radical," political forces well into liberal-left and social democratic circles are impeding progress in the fight against race-based super-exploitation.

3   Conclusion

The starting point of this chapter was to examine the intertwined dynamics of racism in Germany and the European migration and border regime in recent decades. This examination was conducted from the perspective of a materialist theory of domination. The results of this analysis are as follows: The resurgence of racism in Germany can be attributed, at least in part, to social and political defeats suffered by racist forces as a result of anti-racist struggles, the emergence of 'post-migrant' societies, progressive-neoliberal migration policies and the so-called summer of migration. In this context, a growing section of the German population employs racism as a strategy to address their psychological pathologies as subjects damaged by neoliberal policies. Racism is also deployed to defend material advantages in the global distribution of social surplus through restrictive border regimes and to enable the ongoing super-exploitation of labor that is racialized and disenfranchised by migration policies. The upsurge of racism which is fed by these dynamics has resulted in a restrictively tightened migration and border policy.

This thesis-based argumentation demonstrates the analytical productivity of a historical-materialist concept of relations of domination as relations of re/production. Racist relations of domination comprise many elements, including discourses, symbolic orders and language. However, if the character of racism as a relation of domination in the material and social re/production of human life is not included in critical analyses, an emancipatory understanding of racism seems difficult to achieve.

Bibliography

Adorno, Theodor W. (2000) *Einleitung in die Soziologie*. Stanford, CA: Stanford University Press.

Adorno, Theodor W. (2018) *Minima Moralia: Reflections from Damaged Life*. London: Verso.

Adorno, Theodor W. (2019) *The Authoritarian Personality*. London: Verso.

Balibar, Ètienne and Immanuel Wallerstein (1988) *Race Nation Class. Ambiguous Identities*. London and New York: Verso.

Bhattacharya, Tithi (2017) *Social Reproduction Theory: Remapping Class, Recentering Oppression*. London: Pluto Press.

Bojadžijev, Manuela (2006) Migration und Kämpfe. Perspektiven des Rassismus, *Jungle World*, Nov. 22, jungle.world/artikel/2006/47/migration-und-kaempfe.

Bonilla-Silva, Eduardo (2014) *Racism Without Racists. Color-Blind Racism and the Persistence of Racial Inequality in America*. Lanham: Rowman & Littlefield.

Bonilla-Silva, Eduardo (2001) *White Supremacy and Racism in the Post-Civil Rights Era*. Boulder, CO. and London: Lynne Rienner Publishers.

Brand, Ulrich and Markus Wissen (2017) *Imperiale Lebensweise. Zur Ausbeutung von Mensch und Natur im globalen Kapitalismus*. München: oekom Verlag.

Brenkert, George C. (2010) *Marx's Ethics of Freedom*. London and New York: Routledge.

Buckel, Sonja (2015) Dirty Capitalism. In: Dirk Martin et al. (eds.), *Perspektiven und Konstellationen kritischer Theorie*. Münster: Verlag Westfälisches Dampfboot.

Camfield, David (2016) Elements of a Historical-Materialist Theory of Racism, *Historical Materialism*, vol. 24, no. 1, pp. 31–70, DOI: 10.1163/1569206X-12341453.

Decker, Oliver and Elmar Brähler (2020) *Autoritäre Dynamiken. Alte Ressentiments – neue Radikalität. Leipziger Autoritarismus Studie 2020*. Gießen: Psychosozial Verlag.

Dörre, Klaus et al. (2018) Arbeiterbewegung von rechts? Motive und Grenzen einer imaginären Revolte, *Berliner Journal für Soziologie*, vol. 28, pp. 55–89, doi: 10.1007/s11609-018-0352-z.

Espahangizi, Kijan et al. (2016) Rassismus in der postmigrantischen Gesellschaft. Zur Einleitung, *movements. Journal for Critical Migration and Border Regime Studies*, vol. 2, no. 1.

Fraser, Nancy (2017) Für eine neue Linke oder: Das Ende des progressiven Neoliberalismus, *Blätter für deutsche und internationale Politik*, vol. 2, pp. 71–76, blaetter.de/ausgabe/2017/februar/fuer-eine-neue-linke-oder-das-ende-des-progressiven-neoliberalismus.

Georgi, Fabian (2022) Autonomie in der Festung. Grundlagen einer materialistischen Migrations- und Grenzregimeanalyse am Beispiel der EU-Migrationspolitik seit 2015. In: Valeria Hänsel et al. (eds.), *Von Moria bis Hanau – Brutalisierung und Widerstand. Grenzregime IV*. Berlin and Hamburg: Assoziation A, 2022.

Georgi, Fabian (2019a) Kämpfe der Migration im Kontext. Die Krisendynamik des europäischen Grenzregimes seit 2011. In: Daniel Keil and Jens Wissel (eds.), *Staatsprojekt Europa. Eine staatstheoretische Perspektive auf die Europäische Union*. Baden-Baden: Nomos Verlag.

Georgi, Fabian (2019b) The Role of Racism in the European 'Migration Crisis.' A Historical Materialist Perspective. In: Vishwas Satgar (ed.), *Racism After Apartheid. Challenges for Marxism and Anti-Racism*. Johannesburg: Wits University Press.

Georgi, Fabian (2019c) Toward Fortress Capitalism: The Restrictive Transformation of Migration and Border Regimes as a Reaction to the Capitalist Multi-Crisis, *Canadian Review of Sociology*, vol. 56, no. 4, pp. 567–72, DOI: 10.1111/cars.12264.

Goldschmidt, Werner (2004) Herrschaft. In: Wolfgang Fritz Haug et al. (eds.), *Historisch-kritisches Wörterbuch des Marxismus*, Bd 6.1. Hamburg: Argument Verlag.

Hall, Stuart (1980) Race, Articulation and Societies Structured in Dominance. In: UNESCO (ed.), *Sociological Theories: Race and Colonialism*. Paris: UNESCO.

Hoffmann, Marie (2021) Nach dem Sommer. Eine historisch-materialistische Analyse migrationspolitischer Kämpfe in Deutschland nach 2016, *movements. Journal for Critical Migration and Border Regime Studies*, vol. 6, no. 1.

Lessenich, Stephan (2018) Grenzen der Ausbeutung. Wie der globale Norden über die Verhältnisse des Südens lebt. In: Maximilian Becker and Mathilda Reinicke (eds.), *Anders wachsen!* München: oekom Verlag.

Marx, Karl (1996) Capital: A Critique of Political Economy, Volume 1. In Karl Marx and Frederick Engels, *Collected Works Vol. 35*. London: Lawrence and Wishart.

Marx, Karl (1987) The German Ideology. In: Karl Marx and Frederick Engels, *Collected Works Vol. 5*. London: Lawrence and Wishart.

Marz, Ulrike (2017) Annäherungen an eine Kritische Theorie des Rassismus, PERIPHERIE – *Politik, Ökonomie, Kultur*, vol. 37, DOI: 10.3224/peripherie.v37i2.06.

Narr, Wolf-Dieter and Dirk Vogelskamp (2012) *Trotzdem: Menschenrechte! Versuch, uns und anderen nach nationalsozialistischer Herrschaft Menschenrechte zu erklären*. Köln: Komitee für Grundrechte und Demokratie.

Narr, Wolf-Dieter (2015) *Niemands-Herrschaft. Eine Einführung in die Schwierigkeiten Herrschaft zu begreifen.* Hamburg, VSA Verlag.

Rodney, Walter (2018) *How Europe Underdeveloped Africa.* London: Verso.

Roldán Mendívil, Eleonora and Bafta Sarbo (2021) Materialistischer Antirassismus – zurück zu den Wurzeln. In: Judith Dellheim et al. (eds.): *Auf den Schultern von Karl Marx.* Münster: Westfälisches Dampfboot, pp. 297–309.

Spehr, Christoph (2003) *Gleicher als andere: Eine Grundlegung der freien Kooperation.* Berlin: Karl Dietz Verlag.

Statistisches Bundesamt. 2020. Bevölkerung mit Migrationshintergrund – Ergebnisse des Mikrozensus 2019, *Statistisches Bundesamt*, Wiesbaden, destatis.de/DE/Themen/Gesellschaft-Umwelt/Bevoelkerung/Migration-Integration/Publikationen/Downloads-Migration/migrationshintergrund-2010220197004.pdf?__blob=publicationFile.

CHAPTER 5

Intersectionality, Identity, and Marxism

Eleonora Roldán Mendívil and Bafta Sarbo

Intersectionality was first introduced to the social sciences in 1989 by the lawyer Kimberlé Crenshaw.[1] In recent years, the triumph of intersectionality theory has also spread to large parts of German research on gender and racism. However, these approaches are also very popular in political education work on feminism and anti-racism. Intersectionality intends to draw attention to the interaction of different forms of oppression. Especially in the field of anti-discrimination work and in the context of diversity competence, an intersectional approach has become indispensable.

The term not only appears in the German government's coalition agreement in the call for an "intersectional equality policy," (Bundesregierung, 2022: 108) but even Chancellor Olaf Scholz described himself as an "intersectional feminist" during the election campaign (SPD-Parteivorstand, 2021). If even the (neo-)liberal federal government can agree on this term, then from a Marxist perspective, questions arise regarding the socio-critical content of this concept. After all, the explanation for the necessity of intersectionality often does not go beyond the mere statement that categories such as class, gender and *race* are somehow connected and mutually determined. The impetus for our intervention arises from the necessity for a Marxist analysis of the current debates on intersectionality and the integration of this analysis into questions of immanent critique of the Marxist left in Germany. The objective is to make the English-language discussions accessible to a German-speaking audience.

1 History of Origin and the Class Concept

We want to draw on two central texts of the intersectionality debate to briefly summarize their arguments and embed them in their context of origin. Even if the genesis of intersectionality as a category or as a theoretical approach has broader starting points, these two texts are repeatedly cited in all basic

---

1 This article is based on Roldán Mendívil and Sarbo, 2021: 61–71. We would like to thank Hannah Fröhlich for helpful comments and criticism on this article.

discussions. A closer examination with the focus on the class concept utilized in each case enables to approach these texts from a dialectical-materialist perspective and thus derive the foundations of our critique.

The concept of intersecting forms of oppression was first introduced by US lawyer Kimberlé Crenshaw at the Chicago Legal Symposium in 1988 (Bohrer, 2019: 83). Her paper was published the following year (Crenshaw, 2019: 143–184). According to Crenshaw, the experiences of Black women in the US are neither determined solely by being Black nor solely by being a woman. Rather, the interaction between racism and sexism must be understood. Crenshaw illuminated the manner in which US jurisprudence at the time adjudicated cases involving discrimination based on gender and *race* concurrently. One of the court rulings Crenshaw examined involved a lawsuit brought by Black women workers against their dismissal by General Motors. Due to the seniority principle, which affords senior employees greater protection against termination, Black women were dismissed disproportionately often (Ibid: 147). The judge dismissed the case on the grounds that neither black men nor white women were dismissed and therefore neither racial nor sexist discrimination could be proven. The legal challenge, then, was to problematize the US anti-discrimination laws of the time, which only considered gender and *race* separately as legal grounds for discrimination. Therefore, according to Crenshaw, the experiences of Black and other non-white women were ignored by the law. Crenshaw uses the term intersection to describe a situation that we can imagine metaphorically as a traffic junction where gender and *race* intersect. In the event of an accident, it is challenging to determine whether it was caused by the axis of gender or *race*, or even both (Ibid: 158).

A few years before Crenshaw, the Combahee River Collective (CRC) had published the "Combahee River Collective Statement" in Boston in April 1977. The authors of this manifesto were the Black lesbian socialists Demita Frazier and the sisters Barbara and Beverly Smith. Their experiences as Black people, as women and as lesbians moved them to analyze "interlocking oppression (Taylor, 2017: 4)." The CRC saw itself as part of a Marxist tradition[2] and formulated the goal of expanding it to include an understanding of the particular oppression of Black women in the US during the 1970s (Ibid: 7).

The CRC identified as part of the socialist movement and explicitly formulated the claim to represent a specific experience within the working class,

---

2 The end of the manifesto states: "We are socialists because we believe that work must be organized for the collective benefit of those who do the work and create the products, and not for the profit of the bosses. Material resources must be equally distributed among those who create these resources (Taylor, 2017: 19–20)."

namely that of Black women. The CRC statement begins by asserting: "We are actively committed to struggling against racial, sexual, heterosexual, and class oppression."[3] Over the course of the manifesto, the organization makes clear its commitment to socialist revolution. However, the specifics of this revolution remain unclear. For instance, it is not clear who is the revolutionary subject, what is the role of a revolutionary party, or what role do trade unions play. Moreover, a socialist claim is insufficient to the collective:

> We are not convinced, however, that a socialist revolution that is not also a feminist and antiracist revolution will guarantee our liberation. We have arrived at the necessity for developing an understanding of class relationships that takes into account the specific class position of Black women who are generally marginal in the labor force.
> TAYLOR, 2017: 20

These considerations can be understood primarily in the context of the US left of the 1970s. The understanding of class by the majority of socialists at the time meant that socialist politics often took little account in theory and practice of the specific phenomena of super-exploitation as manifested in female and/or non-white or immigrant people. At the same time, socialist politics took place primarily in unionized workplaces and at universities. Women and/or non-white people were thus addressed as workers or students, but the specific ways in which they experienced class and how these population groups experienced above-average precarity and specific forms of disenfranchisement were only marginally addressed. This does not mean that socialist politics in the US in the 1970s only addressed white men, it does however point to gaps that are formulated in the CRC statement. In addition, in the US of the 1970s, the category of Black woman was essentially synonymous with working-class woman. Crenshaw also speaks specifically of a Black underclass and of a targeted political agenda that places Black women from the lowest economic strata at the center of their own politics (Crenshaw, 2019: 183). In her contribution, she does not use her examples to describe the experience of Black women in general, but that of Black women workers in particular. They found themselves in the concrete situation of separate exposure to the arbitrariness of the company

---

3 Taylor (2017: 15). Interestingly, the 2019 German translation reads "against racist, sexist, heterosexist and classist oppression" (Kelly, 2019: 48). This shows how class oppression is translated from English into "classist oppression" and thus the class character of the collective – which saw itself as a Marxist collective of women workers for women workers – is reduced in the German translation to issues of discriminatory treatment based on class affiliation.

and the state. The CRC, too, employs a class concept in which class is only understood as one form of oppression among many others. The contradiction between labor and capital remains obscured, because neither the CRC nor Crenshaw address class issues in the sense of antagonistic property relations in their contributions, as we do as Marxists.[4] In its place is a self-understanding that centers and consequently essentializes the category of Black woman, since belonging to the working class was already assumed conceptually for Black women.[5]

2   Historical Context to the US Left

Both the CRC and Crenshaw build on a number of earlier US debates about the relationship between different forms of oppression. In her monograph *Marxism and Intersectionality* Ashley J. Bohrer (2019) discusses this history. From the dual or triple oppression approach advocated by the Third World Women's Alliance, to the standpoint theory that emerged in the 1970s, particularly in feminist circles, to specific analyses and critiques of Latina feminism, various theories and political experiences have contributed to the shaping of the concept of intersectionality (Ibid: 56–71). Bohrer illustrates how prominent theorists such as Patricia Hill Collins, Angela Davis, bell hooks, and Audre Lorde repeatedly addressed class and, to varying degrees, the struggle against capitalism, although their ideas of who constitutes the subject of liberation and what exactly the theories and projects of liberation look like sometimes differ greatly (Ibid: 71–78).

However, it also raises questions that can be understood as a meaningful extension of class struggle perspectives. In a 1997 essay, Robin D. G. Kelley writes that while identity politics arising from intersectionality theories sometimes hinder genuine alliances, the notion of class would also be enriched by an understanding of alliances and solidarity (Kelley, 1997).

In her article "A Marxist Case for Intersectionality," Sharon Smith argues for a separate consideration of intersectionality as a concept and intersectionality

---

[4] In academic circles and relevant parts of the radical left, class is understood today primarily as classism. For Marxist critiques of the concept of classism, see Hezel and Güßmann, 2021: 41–50; Nehring, 2021: 175–82.

[5] It must be added that although the gradual emergence of a Black petty bourgeoisie up to a considerable Black bourgeoisie could already be observed in the 1970s, it was nowhere near the strength that a "Black super-elite in politics, sport and entertainment" was to achieve in recent decades (Editors, 2022).

theory as an analytical lens (Smith, 2017). The concept is useful, she argues, because it simply demonstrates descriptively the real interlocking of different forms of oppression and because this concept stems from the struggles of Black feminism, from which Marxists as a whole have much to learn about the relationship between class, gender and *race*. However, the analytical lens of intersectionality as a theory with a postmodern political agenda is problematic, as it is associated with a number of neoliberal projects that focus primarily on issues of balanced political representation, for example. According to Smith, the politics of the socialist CRC can serve as a basis for a necessary engagement of Marxists with issues of gender, sexuality and *race*.

However, Barbara Foley argues: If class, gender and *race* are analytical categories, the question is whether they are similar or different in kind. Can they be categorized in a hierarchy or are they fundamentally equivalent to each other (Foley, 2018)? Foley emphasizes that class, gender and *race* require very different analytical approaches to their determination. The distinction between oppression and exploitation is fundamental to Marxist analyses:

> That is, "race" does not cause racism; gender does not cause sexism. But the ways in which "race" and gender – as modes of oppression – have historically been shaped by the division of labor can and should be understood within the explanatory framework supplied by class analysis.
> Ibid

Therefore, in the following section we will focus on analyzing reification in the context of the formation of rigid and politicized identities, which enables a distinction between exploitation, oppression and discrimination from a Marxist perspective.

3 Reification and Identity Politics

Initially, intersectionality was conceived as a means of problematizing one-sided identities. However, in the context of intersectionality theory, the logic of identity politics is not broken up but rather implemented more consistently. The intersectionality approach does not question the preconditions and functioning of identity categories. It begins with people's immediate experiences, – whether they are white men or black women – without addressing the preconditions for the emergence and continued existence of these categories. In this respect, it was unsurprisingly important to the CRC to differentiate their identities as Black lesbian women from those of white men in the left and in the labor movement. The question of how the fractionalization of wage earners produces different experiences within the working class through a progressive division of labor is not addressed by intersectionality theorists. The findings are typically reduced to the banal observation that people's experiences in different social realities are, after all, different. In this context, intersectionality is actually not a theory, but an approach, a lens that problematizes broad categories such as woman, black or migrant on an empirical basis. However, anti-discrimination law, the root of intersectionality theory, holds on to categories that describe unequal treatment. The subject of laws is neither how inequality comes about nor how it functions. This demonstrates the necessity to differentiate between exploitation, oppression, and discrimination, which exemplifies the shortcomings of the intersectionality approach from a Marxist perspective.

Although the CRC refers conceptually to exploitation and oppression, it does not result in an economic definition of their class concept. On the contrary, it is precisely such reification of social categories that is reflected in their class concept. Class is understood less as a relation of exploitation than as an identity constituted through experience.[6] In the Marxist sense, however, class is not simply an identity based on experience. Rather, class is the social relation that ensures the production and accumulation of capital. In bourgeois society, social activity is always reified in categories. The social relations that set the members of a society in relation to each other in their activity thus become fixed characteristics of people or groups. This can be observed, for instance, in the functioning of racism, which conceals the relation between exploitation and super-exploitation in terms of skin color or cultural characteristics.[7] This phenomenon can also be observed in patriarchal orders that reify the relation between production and reproduction as a relation between men and women.[8] While same-sex sexuality between males, for instance, was still regarded as sodomy (something you do) in the European Middle Ages, it has been designated as homosexuality (something you are) at the latest since the advent of modernity (Foucault, 1988). Through identities, people in bourgeois society thus consider their social activity as a characteristic. In *The German Ideology*, Marx contrasts such reification with a communist society in which people's activity does not define them in the form of identity categories:

---

6 This also explains why the German translation of the CRC manifesto speaks of classism instead of class.
7 See the article by Bafta Sarbo in this volume, pp. 16–35.
8 See the article by Eleonora Roldán Mendívil and Hannah Vögele in this volume, pp. 36–50.

[W]hereas in communist society, where nobody has one exclusive sphere of activity but each can become accomplished in any branch he wishes, society regulates the general production and thus makes it possible for me to do one thing today and another tomorrow, to hunt in the morning, fish in the afternoon, rear cattle in the evening, criticise after dinner, just as I have a mind, without ever becoming hunter, fisherman, shepherd or critic.

MARX, 1976: 47

Capitalist and worker are also not simply identities characterized by the possession of money or lack thereof. Rather, they stand in a specific relation to each other, in which the wealth of the one is founded on the poverty and dispossession of the other. This is why capitalism also requires so-called original accumulation, the historical process by which the working class is created in the first place through the systematic and violent separation of the producers from their means of production (Marx, 1996: 744). The relevant aspect here is that the propertylessness of the working class is not only the result, but rather the precondition of the relation between capital and labor. This means that workers are not only poor because they are exploited, rather they can only be exploited because they are poor. Nevertheless, this also gives rise to the specific power of the working class in the process of social production. The fact that social wealth is produced by their labor also implies that they have the capacity to halt production. The class consciousness of the working class, that is, the identification with the class, is the realization of its power as a collective historical subject on which social life depends. This consciousness as self-understanding is not a static identity, rather is formed in the context of political struggle where the experience of this power is actualized. In intersectionality theory, these questions of power and social change should lead to a critique on a structural level, but in practice they are typically negotiated at the interpersonal level. The Marxist-feminist theorist Delia Aguilar notes that in this analysis, class is not even a category of agency (Foley, 2018). For example, the aforementioned essay by Crenshaw deals with a legal process of women workers, who only appear as Black female individuals. Their class position as workers does not confer upon them the capacity to act collectively and fight for their equality.

Furthermore, within the concept of intersectionality, womanhood and Blackness are not each localized as contingent on the constantly changing conditions of a class society, but ultimately they are rather perceived as static positions of oppression. This seemingly negligible weakness forms the basis for both an idealist and positivist approach to identity. Instead of a historically evolved relation, we are presented with positivist assignments of marginalized identities as a response to real oppression. The relationship between capital and labor that underlies this oppression thus remains obscured.

The characterization of class as a relation of exploitation differs from oppression as a political relation – expressed in terms of gender or *race*, for example – and discrimination as an analytical category. As a legal category, discrimination according to the General Act on Equal Treatment (AGG) of 2006 exists when there is an immediate (direct or overt) disadvantage, meaning when a person is treated less favorably compared to another person (Federal Anti-Discrimination Agency). The characteristics may vary considerably: from a migration background to sexual orientation or the position of a part-time employee within a company.

For us, however, discrimination is analytically a distinct from oppression. Discrimination describes a generic term for disparate treatment based on various social norms. Discrimination can occur even in the absence of structural relations of mediation such as *race*, usually in conjunction with disadvantageous treatment. If non-migrant children are referred to as "German potatoes" in schools attended by a majority of immigrant children, they experience a form of group-based discrimination. In this specific school context, they face a discriminatory situation as a minority; they cannot help the absence of a migrant background. However, they do not experience oppression. This is because in order to move from discrimination to a relation of oppression, it requires the overall social, structural disadvantage of said group. However, non-immigrant Germans in Germany are not structurally disadvantaged or marginalized as a group in any way. Structurally, the opposite is true. Consequently, discrimination can evolve into a structural form of oppression that mediates various capital relations, however, the recognition of discrimination in general does not indicate oppression in particular.

4   The Political Economy of Intersectionality

While intersectionality initially aimed to describe the specifics of Black women's experiences in contrast to those of Black men and white women, the approach is now understood in a more individualized manner. Discrimination or privilege categories intersect in each person, providing each person with a set of identities. Such an understanding of intersectionality thus enables a more compartmentalized categorization of identity and therefore a constantly intensifying and fragmenting form of identity politics. Intersectionality theorist Leslie McCall also argues that "intersectionality is [a] broadly applicable theory, with insights for multiple spheres of life, and with implications for diagnosing inequality and identity *generally* rather than of black women *specifically* (Bohrer, 2019: 87)."

While both Crenshaw and the CRC refer to working-class Black women, there is a key distinction between the movement-oriented CRC and Crenshaw's intersectionality as a form of anti-discrimination politics. The concept of intersectionality gained prominence at a time when socialist politics were losing ground. The state became increasingly the addressee of political demands (Lent and Trumann, 2015). The question of equality is no longer discussed as a strategic intermediate step towards general human liberation, but as the goal of the struggle itself. For instance, governmental equal treatment directives and the phenomenon of gender mainstreaming can be understood as forms of state-sanctioned feminism that do not challenge or fight patriarchal oppression, but rather strive for a proportional representation of women without questioning the basis of this oppression, namely the relation between capital and labor. Walter Benn Michaels (2009), for example, posits that "increasing tolerance of economic inequality and increasing intolerance of racism, sexism and homophobia [...] are fundamental characteristics of neoliberalism."

According to Foley, intersectionality is therefore not a useful analytical framework, but an ideological expression of our time (Foley, 2018). The popularity and further development of this approach in the social sciences can only be understood as an expression of social change. The new modes of production in post-Fordism, which place new demands on labor, could offer an explanation for this. The migration of industrial production to countries in the Global South has led to the emergence of a service-based economy in the former industrialized nations. While Fordism was still based on extensive automation and the equalization of production conditions, in recent years a form of production has prevailed in which workers are challenged more strongly as subjects (Voß, 2007: 97–113). Employees who can and should make use of their personal experience as a specific competence in their work process are increasingly in demand. The current form that neoliberalism has assumed worldwide is characterized, among other things, by the integration of subjectivity into the work process.

The popularity of concepts such as diversity must therefore be understood in the context of capital's changing demands of labor. Bourgeois anti-racism therefore always understands racism as a locational disadvantage for German capital: "Migration is [...] generally a positive selection anyway; for it tends to be less the fearful, indecisive, risk-averse and insufficiently qualified who leave, and more the courageous, decisive, risk-taking and qualified (Bade, 2013: 73)." The criticism of racism from this perspective is a rational one that has economic development in mind: "Germany has always been a country full of diversity. This has been even more true since 1945, when Europe also learned to understand its diversity as wealth (Böhmer, 2007: 17–22)."

Postmodernity as an era is characterized by the rejection of grand narratives (Jameson, 1991). It is now dominant in various disciplines of the critical social sciences. Its popularity can be explained by the combination of critical habitus and liberal theoretical premises. It can also be understood as a theoretical expression of the differentiated realities of life under neoliberalism. In contrast, Marxism, from which postmodernism distinguishes itself, represents a universal socialist standpoint. This is not in the sense of an abstract universalism that postulates colorblindness and abstract equality, but one that permeates the dialectic of the general and the particular. This is substantiated by Eve Mitchell:

> Patriarchal and racialized social relations are material, concrete and real. So are the contradictions between the particular and universal, and the appearance and essence. The solution must build upon these contradictions and push on them.
> MITCHELL, 2013

However, it is precisely this dialectic that has been mostly neglected in recent decades of the socialist movement. Intersectionality thus emerged at a time when many of the everyday problems surrounding real relations of violence were not sufficiently addressed by socialists or were insufficiently explained and combated. Intersectionality is therefore also a response to a real labor movement and its shortcomings.

Mitchell builds upon Frantz Fanon's assertion that he is both a human being and a Black man, positing that: "'I am a woman and a human' [...] The key is to emphasize both sides of the contradiction." This simultaneity of generality and particular experience allows Marxist theory to analyze the specific circumstances of various segments of the working class while avoiding the pitfalls of categorically fragmenting and essentializing social differences. Vivek Chibber also takes up this point in his critique of postcolonialism, a particular theoretical strand of postmodernism, and emphasizes the centrality of universalism in Marxist theory. Postcolonial theoretical approaches reject a Marxist standpoint, arguing that it unjustifiably projects the experiences and categories of the Global North or of white men onto marginalized groups. According to Chibber, this not only ignores the fact that the majority of people who oriented themselves towards Marxism in the 20th century and developed it further were not white, but also two central universalisms that have a special explanatory power: the universalization of the logic of capital, which extends as a law to all areas of society, and the universality of resistance to it, which arises from the general human need not to live in subjugation (Chibber, 2013).

A Marxist analysis takes the exploitation of the working class as the central moment of capitalist production and can describe the specifics of different parts of the class from this starting point without rejecting the general. Foregrounding the question of exploitation does not imply that relations of oppression are not also relevant for the analysis of capitalism. Exploitation explains how profits are generated from the labor of those who produce things, that is, how capital is created.

According to Barbara Foley, "we need to ask not only what kinds of questions it [intersectionality theory] encourages and remedies, but also what kinds of questions it discourages and what kinds of remedies it forecloses." She concludes by stating: "Although intersectionality can usefully describe the effects of multiple oppressions [...] it does not offer an adequate explanatory framework for addressing the root causes of social inequality in the capitalist socioeconomic system (Foley, 2018)."

A socialist self-understanding or the representation of experiences within the working class therefore does not yet imply a Marxist method: as previously demonstrated, both the CRC and later Kimberlé Crenshaw, who no longer formulates a socialist claim, treat class, if at all, as a mere additional form of oppression, rather than as a relation of economic exploitation in class societies. The material basis of categories such as gender, sexuality, and *race* is therefore not understood, and class cannot be seen as the starting point of a collective subjectivity. Being a worker is just another identity and the unique revolutionary potential of the position of direct and indirect wage earners in the re/production process disappears.

5 Conclusion

From the outset, the intersectionality concept has equated exploitation and oppression, thus contributing to a theory in which class in the form of class discrimination is one form of discrimination among many, which can ultimately be unlearned through anti-prejudice pedagogy in the same way as (hetero)sexist, racist or trans-hostile attitudes (Camfield, 2016: 45).

Capitalism itself produces the reification of identity: categories such as black, brown or immigrant are reified in an essentialist manner, rather than being located as a momentary social relation within a concrete and constantly changing reality. Consequently, the meaning of the term is contingent upon the context, whether in the United States or in Germany. Intersectionality theory is a dead end because it reduces different social relations to oppression and identity issues. Intersectionalists fail to challenge the historical development and social functioning of identities and consequently fail to relate them to the underlying class relations of exploitation. As a result, they fail to develop a perspective that recognizes the necessity to overcome these relations.

Although this perspective is often espoused in theory, in practice we observe that even liberal factions of capital, as represented by the current federal government, employ the intersectionality approach. The fact that class relations are the fundamental material structure of our society is obscured, as is the resulting need to attack the economic base in order to "overthrow all relations in which man is a debased, enslaved, abandoned, despicable essence (Marx, 1844)." Both economic exploitation and the forms of political and ideological oppression that arise from it and have an effect on it must be included in this upheaval. It is important to differentiate between the different ways in which class and gender, sexuality and *race* function to avoid abandoning the emancipatory claim of the liberation of humanity as a whole. In order to develop a politics that does not pit exploitation against oppression, but rather understands and addresses them in relation to each other, it requires analyses that understand and politicize gender, sexuality and racism structurally in the context of capitalist relations of exploitation. This also requires a socialist left that is willing to engage in self-criticism, to acknowledge its own mistakes and shortcomings, rather than merely locating the problems externally. Only on such a basis can a truly dialectical understanding of Marxist critique emerge (McNally, 2017: 94–95).

While intersectionality theory, which originated in the US, has been widely adopted in Germany, the criticism of it that has been formulated in the English-speaking world for many years has received little attention. With our contribution, we aim to provide the German-speaking public with an understanding of these debates, which are by no means limited to a blanket rejection of every intersectionality approach. Rather, they prompt us to examine more closely the ideas of society, class and political struggles that are actually associated with these approaches.

Bibliography

Bade, Klaus J. (2013) Kritik und Gewalt. Sarrazin-Debatte, "Islamkritik" und Terror in der Einwanderungsgesellschaft. Schwalbach: Wochenschau Verlag.

Böhmer, Maria (2007) Für eine Kultur der Vielfalt in Wirtschaft, Gesellschaft und Staat. In: Daniel Dettling and Julia Gerometta (eds.), Vorteil Vielfalt. Herausforderungen und Perspektiven einer offenen Gesellschaft. Wiesbaden: VS Verlag für Sozialwissenschaften.

Bohrer, Ashley J. (2019) Marxism and Intersectionality. Race, Gender, Class and Sexuality under Contemporary Capitalism. Bielefeld: Transcript Verlag.

Bundesregierung (2022) Coalition Agreement 2021 – 2025 between the Social Democratic Party of Germany (SPD), Alliance 90/The Greens and the Free Democrats (FDP), Jan 11, italia.fes.de/fileadmin/user_upload/German_Coalition_Treaty_2021-2025.pdf.

Crenshaw, Kimberlé (2019) Das Zusammenwirken von Race und Gender ins Zentrum rücken: Eine Schwarze feministische Kritik des Antidiskriminierungsdogmas, der feministischen Theorie und antirassistischer Politiken. In: Natasha A. Kelly (ed.), Schwarzer Feminismus. Grundlagentexte Münster: Unrast Verlag.

Camfield, David (2016) Elements of a Historical-Materialist Theory of Racism, Historical Materialism, vol. 24, no. 1, pp. 31–70, DOI: 10.1163/1569206X-12341453.

Chibber, Vivek (2013) Postcolonial Theory and the Specter of Capital. London: Verso.

Editors (2022) EXCERPT: Black Bourgeoisie, Black Agenda Review, Jan 12, blackagendareport.com/excerpt-black-bourgeoisie.

Federal Anti-Discrimination Agency. What is discrimination? antidiskriminierungsstelle.de/EN/about-discrimination/what-is-discrimination/what-is-discrimination-node.html.

Foley, Barbara (2018) Intersectionality: A Marxist Critique, Portside, portside.org/2018-10-31/intersectionality-marxist-critique.

Foucault, Michel (1988) The History of Sexuality, Vol. 1: We "Other Victorians." New York: Vintage Books.

Hezel, Lena and Steffen Güßmann (2021) ‚Klassismus' – Diskussion ohne Klassenanalyse? Zeitschrift Z. Marxistische Erneuerung, vol. 126, pp. 41–50.

Jameson, Frederic (1991) Postmodernism or the Cultural Logic of Late Capitalism. Durham: Duke University Press.

Kelley, Robin D. G. (1997) Identity Politics and Class Struggle, Libcom, libcom.org/library/identity-politics-class-struggle.

Kelly, Natasha A. (2019) Schwarzer Feminismus. Grundlagentexte Münster: Unrast Verlag.

Lent, Lilli and Andrea Trumann (2015) Kritik des Staatsfeminismus. Berlin: Bertz und Fischer.

Marx, Karl (1996) Capital: A Critique of Political Economy, Volume 1. In Karl Marx and Frederick Engels, Collected Works Vol. 35. London: Lawrence and Wishart.

Marx, Karl (1844) Introduction to A Contribution to the Critique of Hegel's Philosophy of Right. In: German-French Annals, February 7 and 10, marxists.org/archive/marx/works/1843/critique-hpr/intro.htm.

Marx, Karl (1976) The German Ideology. In: Karl Marx and Frederick Engels, Collected Works Vol. 5. London: Lawrence and Wishart.

McNally, David (2017) Intersections and Dialectics: Critical Reconstructions in Social Reproduction Theory. In: Tithi Bhattacharya (ed.), Social Reproduction Theory. Remapping Class, Recentering Oppression. London: Verso.

Michaels, Walter Benn (2009) What Matters, London Review of Books, Aug 27, www.lrb.co.uk/the-paper/v31/n16/walter-benn-michaels/what-matters.

Mitchell, Eve (2013) I Am a Woman and a Human: A Marxist-Feminist Critique of Intersectionality Theory, Unity and Struggle, unityandstruggle.org/2013/09/i-am-a-woman-and-a-human-a-marxist-feminist-critique-of-intersectionality-theory/.Vib.

Nehring, Fabian (2021) Klassismus: Ideologiekritik als Ideologie, Widerspruch. Beiträge zur sozialistischen Politik, vol. 77, pp. 175–82, widerspruch.ch/sites/default/files/2021-10/77_Nehring_Klassismus.pdf.

Smith, Sharon (2017) "A Marxist case for intersectionality," *Socialist Worker*, socialistworker.org/2017/08/01/a-marxist-case-for-intersectionality.

SPD-Parteivorstand, *Twitter*, March 6, 2021, twitter.com/spdde/status/1368149358378508290?lang=en.

Taylor, Keeanga-Yamahtta (2017) *How We Get Free. Black Feminism and the Combahee River Collective*. Chicago: Haymarket Books.

Voß, G. Günter (2007) "Subjektivierung von Arbeit und Arbeitskraft. Die Zukunft der Beruflichkeit und die Dimension Gender als Beispiel." In: Brigitte Aulenbacher et. al. (eds.), *Arbeit und Geschlecht im Umbruch der modernen Gesellschaft*. Wiesbaden: VS Verlag für Sozialwissenschaften.

CHAPTER 6

Police and Racism in Germany: A Historical Genesis

Lea Pilone

> The concept of security does not raise civil society above its egoism. On the contrary, security is the *insurance* of its egoism.
> KARL MARX (1987: 164)

∴

Since the Black Lives Matter protests in May 2020 following the murder of George Floyd, there has been an increase in discussions about racist police violence in Germany. Contrary to some reactionary claims, racist police violence is also an everyday occurrence in Germany and by no means a purely US-American problem. The *Death in Custody* campaign has identified 209 deaths of people with a history of migration in German police custody since 1990. According to their research, in 2021 alone six people died at the hands of police officers: Giórgis Zantiotis, Kamal Ibrahim, Abdul I., Omar K., Sivan and Qosay Sadam Khalaf.[1]

The debate is largely dominated by liberal interpretations. These posit that racist police practices are based on implicit and explicit racist attitudes of police officers. Activist contributions also identify the problem in racist stereotypes (Pichl, 2018: 112; Belina, 2018: 120; Autor*innenkollektiv, 2018: 183). However, they go one step further and point out connections that go beyond those stereotypes: the legal basis for action enabling racist police controls in the first place, continuities from colonialism to present-day police, the significance of class and the role of the police in the production of capitalist relations (Autor*innenkollektiv, 2018: 186–87; Thompson, 2018: 198, 204; Samour,

---

1 *Death in Custody* only researches the deaths of "Black people, people of color and people affected by racism" (Death in Custody: Todesfälle in Gewahrhaft, doku.deathincustody.info/). Systematic research on non-immigrants who have died in police custody is not available. It is therefore currently not possible to make any definite statements in this regard.

2017: 13–15; Brazzel, 2017: 25; El-Tayeb and Thompson, 2019: 326; Jawabreh, 2021: 40).

In order to comprehend the origins of racist police violence within the German context, abstract explanations in terms of racial or class affiliation are insufficient. In order to comprehend racist police controls, it is necessary to analyze the position of those controlled within the relations of production and the impact it has on the nature and extent of police controls. In doing so, the connections between the police object, class and the current class composition as well as racism, exploitation and super-exploitation must be brought together.

This is the starting point for this article. It first examines how the police is linked to the emergence of capitalism. The aim is to show the capitalist order's necessities from which the police emerged and their role in the production of capitalist relations. By examining specific historical moments in the history of the German police, the article seeks to establish a connection between the relations of production and the question of who becomes the target of police controls. The aim is to gain insight into why capitalism involves the selective surveillance of certain population groups and why this is particularly evident in poor people with a history of migration in the present day.

1   The Origins of the Police in Europe

Institutional police apparatuses emerged in Europe during the transition from feudalism to capitalism. In what is now Germany, the kingdoms and dynasties issued a number of police ordinances (*Policeyordnungen*) from the 17th and 18th centuries onwards (Härter, 2017: 79–80). Their aim was to establish and maintain security and public order. Early on, a large area was dedicated to criminals who were considered a threat to this public order. These were mainly the poorer classes: Vagabonds, beggars, vagrants, gangs of thieves and robbers or prostitutes (Ibid: 86).

Vagabonds or vagrants were those who wandered through the countryside, had no fixed ties to a place and often slept in the open air. Many of them only became destitute as a result of their violent dispossession through the privatization of land (Marx, 1996: 52). They lacked the means to secure their own livelihood (Neocleous, 2021: 24). They subsided by means of begging, petty theft or other informal activities and were regarded as lazy. Their behavior did not cause much social harm and rarely caused injuries to other people. Nevertheless, they were the focus of policing. Why?

The primary issue was that people who were expected to work for wages did not do so. Bourgeois theorists of the time recognized that labor was essential for the production of wealth, yet they believed that this could only be expected from the poor.[2] In his 1799 text *The State of Indigence*, Scottish police theorist Patrick Colquhoun argued that labor was "absolutely requisite to the existence of all Governments; and it is from the Poor only that labour can be expected (Ibid: 128)." The dispossessed, in turn, posed a constant threat to private property and the capitalist order. Because of their poverty, they were predisposed to attack the private property of others. For some, theft was the only means of securing their own livelihood (Blasius, 1978: 54). Furthermore, the miserable position of the dispossessed harbored the potential that they would turn against the social order, which only provided misery for them. Police concepts were developed on the basis of this insecurity of private property (Neocleous, 2021: 120). For Georg Wilhelm Friedrich Hegel, the issue was not poverty in and of itself, but rather the decline in the living standards of the lower classes below a certain threshold. For then arises a rabble with an attitude that is directed against "the rich, against society, the government etc. (Ibid: 122)." Colquhoun also distinguishes between poverty and indigence (Ibid: 128). He understands poverty as the state in which the individual owns no property and must earn his living through labor. For him, indigence is "the state of any one who is destitute of the means of subsistence, and is unable to labour to procure it to the extent nature requires (Ibid)." For him, indigence is the real "evil," because it is the origin of crime (Ibid: 130). He therefore suggested that the indigent class should be identified by the police and prevented from turning to crime instead of working (Ibid: 128, 130).

Vagrancy presented a challenge to this, as there was no centralized database of individuals at the time. The "work-shy and destitute" individuals could be most effectively controlled at their places of origin, as it was the only location where information about their criminal record could be accessed with ease (Bonillo, 2001: 36–37; Becker, 1992: 118–19). Activities such as begging which guaranteed a livelihood in ways other than wage labor were particularly criminalized. Although such behavior did not directly harm other people, it was considered harmful from a capitalist point of view. It impeded capital accumulation, as it prevented the impoverished masses from working for low wages for the capitalists. As long as such behavior was attractive, the poor had the opportunity to subsist in ways other than wage labor. Instead, they were to be

---

2   Georg Wilhelm Friedrich Hegel noted that the emergence of poverty in general is a consequence of bourgeois society and inevitably results from it (Neocleous, 2021: 122).

disciplined to work. In the German territories, from the 16th century onwards, a distinction was made between beggars who were able to work and those who were unable to work, whereby only those unable to work were considered as genuinely poor (Rusche and Kirchheimer, 2017: 34). All others were labeled as undisciplined, lazy and averse to labor. Being poor and not working despite physical ability was treated as a conscious decision that should be prosecuted (Pilone, 2021).

The criminalization of poverty-based behavior forced the masses into wage labor and educated them for it. By introducing new forms of punishment, the ruling class was able to satisfy capital's need for cheap labor (Rusche and Kirchheimer, 2017: 24). Under mercantilism, corporal and capital punishment gave way to forced labor in penitentiaries or as oarsmen on the galleys, the warships of the Middle Ages and the early modern period.[3]

It created the class of "doubly free" wage laborers, who had "nothing to sell but their own skin (Marx, 1996: 705)." It was indispensable for the emergence of capitalist relations. Without them, no capitalist could exist, because ownership of the means of production alone does not make anyone a capitalist. The capital relation emerges only through the addition of the "doubly free" wage laborer, thereby establishing him as a capitalist (Ibid: 752). The police force was the most important tool for establishing capitalist relations. Without selective criminalization of certain behaviors, they could not have come into being.[4] Thus, historically, the police were not created for the prevention of crime as such, but to prevent a particular class, that of the dispossessed, from becoming criminals instead of working.

2   Control and Criminalization of Foreign Poverty

During the persecution of "criminal vagrants/gangs of thieves and robbers" from the second half of the 17th century onwards, marginalized groups marked as foreign, such as Roma and Sinti and so-called *Betteljuden* (Poor Jews), were increasingly presented as a security threat.[5] Poor Jews were homeless and

---

3   Working as an oarsman on the galleys was extremely feared due to the high mortality rate, which is why even state hunts were organized for vagrants in order to use them as galley slaves as punishment (Rusche and Kirchheimer, 2017: 53–54).
4   For a detailed presentation of this topic, see Weis, 2018.
5   The terms Sinti and Roma are used to describe a group of people who have lived in Europe since the 15th century and originally come from India or Pakistan. Sinti refers to the group that settled in Western and Central Europe, and Roma to the group that settled in Eastern and South-Eastern Europe (Amaro Foro e.V., 2020; Härter, 2017: 86).

indigent Jews who were forced to beg and moved from place to place to find support. In this context, homeless means that they were not officially members of a Jewish community. They became homeless (*heimatlos*) as a result of mass expulsions in connection with the plague from the middle of the 14th century (Kaplan, 2020: 96). A criminal essence was ascribed to Roma and Sinti in particular, who were said to roam as gangs, making a living through theft, robbery and welfare (Bonillo, 2001: 34; Nitschke, 1990: 94). The first records of a Roma presence in German territories date back to 1417 (Frings, 2016: 35). Although they were initially granted letters of safe conduct (*Schutzbriefe*), their expulsion increased with the crises in Europe at the end of the 14th century, such as famine, the plague and wars (Ibid: 38). Subsequent settlement and entry bans, deportations or restrictions on the exercise of trade prevented attempts by Roma and Sinti to settle throughout the early modern period (Ibid: 56). Some of them were therefore actually forced into begging, just like a considerable proportion of the population as a whole (Ibid: 45). Nevertheless, in contrast to the contemporary perception, not all Roma and Sinti were criminals; many made a living from trade, crafts or wage labor, and military service was the most prevalent form of employment for Central and Western European Sinti from the time of the Thirty Years' War until the mid-18th century (Ibid: 46). Nevertheless, the punishments against Roma and Sinti were considerably more severe, which frequently contributed to their social decline (Bonillo, 2001: 34; Fings, 2016: 47). In many German territories, they were prohibited from entering during 18th century and in some instances, they were threatened with the death penalty in the event of infringement.[6]

Controlling the foreign poor was a major concern of police ordinances. There were two main reasons for this. Firstly, the rulers did not want to admit any foreign poor individuals who might potentially become criminals. Secondly, they did not want to have to pay for their care. For instance, in the county of Lippe during the 18th century, sick and foreign beggars were to be turned away at the borders of the villages.[7] In the 17th century, instructions were given to various communities not to accommodate foreign Jewish beggars (Kaplan, 2019: 37). In order to control the influx of foreign beggars and keep them out, towns introduced entry and exit fees as well as checkpoints between the 16th and 18th centuries (Kaplan, 2020: 101–02). During this period, all persons not belonging

---

6 In the duchy of Saxe-Coburg, Roma and Sinti were to be hanged on repeated arrest. In Bavaria, even the first entry into the territory was punishable by death from 1716 (Nitschke, 1990: 45, 94).

7 However, many places lacked the necessary infrastructure for consistent deportation (Ibid: 148).

to a specific community were considered foreign, but marginalized groups such as Roma and Sinti or poor Jews suffered particularly from this attribution and were subject to more rigorous controls. Another area of police activity was therefore the monitoring of poor relief and the exclusion of the foreign poor from these benefits.

The criminalization occurred in an already xenophobic context, but the penal policies added fuel to the fire. The publicly conveyed security threat was used to expand control under criminal law (Bonillo, 2001: 34). For example, the introduction of passports and passport controls to monitor the foreign poor in the 18th century was essential for the establishment of police apparatuses (Nitschke, 1990: 135–36). From the turn of the 20th century, the German Empire began to systematically record Roma and Sinti as part of the modernization of the police. They were measured, photographed and their fingerprints were taken by the dozen without any suspicion of crime (Bonillo, 2001: 151–54). The centralization of data in order to improve the investigation system was essential for their surveillance (Ibid: 151–52). In 1907, when compulsory photographs on the identity documents of Roma and Sinti were being discussed, a district administrator considered whether this should also be introduced for all other residents (Ibid: 153). Interpol, today's most important organization for the coordination of international police work, also has its origins partly in the surveillance of Roma and Sinti. It emerged from the International Criminal Police Commission founded in Vienna in 1923, which created intergovernmental coordination and an exchange of information with regard to the "gypsy problem," among other things (Jain, 2019: 48).

3 Police and Exploitation in the German Colonies

In the colonies, the close connection between the police and wage labor was also evident. The class of wage laborers, which was indispensable for capitalist accumulation, did not yet exist there and first had to be created by police means (Marx, 1996: 752–57). Criminal law became a central instrument for achieving this objective.

In the German colonies, fundamentally different legal systems applied to Europeans and colonized people (Speitkamp, 2021: 61). Enlightenment principles of law did not apply in the colonies: the principle that there can be no penalty without written law (*nulla poena sine lege scripta*) did not apply to the colonized (Ibid: 68–69). Colonial officials were thus able to arbitrarily define offenses such as "insolence," "continued laziness" or "unjustified abandonment" of the workplace (Liebscher, 2021: 160).

Corporal punishment, forced labor, chained imprisonment and death sentences, which were no longer common in Europe, were also applied for the productive use of colonized labor. Georg Rusche and Otto Kirchheimer argue that the type of punishment depends on the needs of capital in the respective relations of production. Although their analysis relates primarily to European developments, it is also relevant to the colonies. Rusche and Kirchheimer (2017: 26) note that in the era of mercantilism from the 16th to the 18th century, labor was scarce and the capitalists could only secure workers on the open market "by paying high wages and granting favorable working conditions." Consequently, they were "obliged to turn to the state" in order to accumulate capital (Ibid). Accordingly, the punishments changed:

> The possibility of exploiting the labor of prisoners now received increasing attention. Galley slavery, deportation, and penal servitude at hard labor were introduced [...] These changes were not the result of humanitarian considerations, but of certain economic developments.
> Ibid: 24

Once the problem of a lack of an industrial reserve army had been resolved and capitalists were able to find workers on the free market at favorable terms, the type of punishment changed to solitary confinement. "The house of correction fell into decay" because free labor could "produce much more," in short "because other and better sources of profit had been found (Ibid: 95)."

A similar situation occurred in the German colonies, where there was hardly any labor willing to work voluntarily for the colonizers. Despite the German Empire's assertion that forced labor would be of greater educational value than imprisonment for the indigenous populations in order to prevent their "aversion [...] to work," punishment in the form of forced labor was also more practical (Steinkröger, 2019: 211). This allowed for the productive use of convict labor in the construction of the colony. Similarly, corporal punishment, which had already been abolished in Europe, was used, partly because it was easier to enforce and partly because the "labor [...] of the convicts would be immediately available again if the corporal punishment was carried out moderately (Ibid: 183)." The legal inequality between Europeans and natives in colonial criminal law ensured the division of labor based on *race*. The colonized population was forced to work as punishment, while European prisoners could be made to work in forced labor, however, "in light of the difficult climatic conditions" this option should be avoided (Ibid: 212). Criminal law and the police thus ensured the super-exploitation of African labor, whose wages were not comparable to those of European workers (Rodney, 2018: 176–77).

When there were only few indigenous workers left in German South West Africa following the genocide of the Herero and Nama between 1904 and 1908, the Landespolizei was deployed to secure the native labor force (Muschalek, 2019: 131). Although the exact tasks of the Landespolizei were not defined, their most important task was to locate, capture and register the native labor force and then monitor and punish them (Ibid: 99, 101). The Landespolizei became an instrument to "hunt down" and capture fugitive native workers and those who were hiding in the outer areas of the colony (Ibid: 137). It coerced those who did not voluntarily participate in the colonial wage economy. Discourses about idleness, lazy natives and those unwilling to work were similar to those during the criminalization of vagabondage in the German Empire. The men and women apprehended by the Landespolizei were either distributed to the farms of the white colonizers or they were subjected to forced labor or chained imprisonment. As additional measures to create a mass of wage laborers, freedom of movement was restricted through passport controls and self-sufficiency was combated through the banning of the ownership of cattle (Liebscher, 2021: 160–61).

German colonialism drove the economic exploitation and impoverishment of its colonies, using the police and their punitive methods to guarantee the best conditions for the exploitation of colonial labor for private enterprise. Thus, when colonial governments spoke of "the maintenance of law and order," they were referring to maintaining the most favorable conditions for the expansion of capitalism and the plundering of the colonies (Rodney, 2018: 196).

4 Racist Criminalization Processes Today

What implications do these historical developments have for the police today, and how do they relate to racist police practices in Germany?

Alongside deportations and *racial profiling*, we observe racist criminalization processes and police practices in Germany when dealing with so-called *Clankriminalität*. Law enforcement agencies understand this to mean "the commission of crimes by members of ethnically segregated structures ('clans')," which they usually locate in families of Turkish or Arab origin (Liebscher, 2020: 535).[8] In this debate, crime is often linked to Turkish, Kurdish or Arab origin and culture in an essentializing way. For example, an internal

---

8 On racist police checks in so-called dangerous or crime-ridden places and on Deutsche Bahn long-distance trains, see Autor*innenkollektiv, 2018: 181–96.

police brochure on "Arab family clans" argues that no distinction should be made between criminal and non-criminal family members, "because basic thought patterns are often also anchored in family members who are not criminally conspicuous."[9] The cause of criminality is culturalized instead of being located in the social conditions from which it arose. The years of exclusion due to employment bans or the suspension of compulsory schooling and the constant insecurity caused by an unsecured residence status, such as the repeated granting of exceptional leave, are not included in the analysis (Rauls and Feltes, 2021: 100).

Racism persists in police work that is linked to the racist connection between origin and criminality. For some years now, the police in major German cities have been pursuing a zero-tolerance strategy or a "policy of a thousand pinpricks" in the fight against clan crime. It is based on the so-called *broken windows theory*, which was developed by US criminologists James Q. Wilson and George L. Kelling. According to this theory, crime and signs of disorder, such as graffiti, a broken window or homelessness, are "inextricably linked (Correia and Wall, 2018: 196)." It follows that the police should intervene at the slightest sign of disorder in order to prevent major crimes (Camp and Heatherton, 2016: 3). They should confront every misdemeanor with "zero tolerance."[10]

This makes *broken windows policing* essentially a modern iteration of early modern *Policeyordnungen*: it is not about detecting a crime or preventing particularly serious crimes, rather, it is about controlling poverty and the resulting behavior. This is because the "zero tolerance" strategy does not imply that the police enforce "law and order" equally everywhere. Police operations with "zero tolerance" against corporate crimes are not on the agenda, even though they cause much greater material damage.[11] Instead, police officers equipped with submachine guns raid hookah bars and other small immigrant businesses in order to identify violations of fire safety, customs regulations or trade regulations. Hardly any real criminals are found during these operations.[12] The

---

9   Dorothee Dienstbühl in a brochure published by the Essen police headquarters for internal training purposes on "Arab family clans – history, analysis, approaches to combating them," as cited in Liebscher, 2020: 539-40.

10 The *broken windows theory* was first put into police practice in 1993 by New York Mayor Rudolph Giuliani and Police Commissioner William Bratton and then exported by neoliberal organizations such as the Manhattan Institute (Weis, 2018: 272; Wacquant, 2009: 265).

11 To illustrate: the German state has lost at least 35.9 billion € through the Cum-ex scandal. The coin that was stolen from the Bode Museum, on the other hand, was only worth 3.75 million € (ZDF heute, 2020; Ackermann et al, 2021). On the overall damage caused by white-collar crime, see Brettel and Schneider, 2021: 73.

12 In the period between May 27 and September of 2019, a total of 197 administrative offences were detected in Berlin by 772 officers, with only 56 cases suspected of being

high-profile raids, which are often reported in advance by the tabloid press in particular, make little sense from an investigative point of view: actual criminal offenses are generally more likely to be proven with covert measures (Rauls and Feltes, 2021: 99). Moreover, these operations are not necessarily an appropriate means to combating organized crime. According to the European police authority Europol, the primary challenge posed by organized crime lies with the Italian mafia and not with Arab clans in Germany (Ibid).

The effect of these police operations varies considerably. On the one hand, the aggressive police raids are part of a gentrification process.[13] The police act as capital's henchmen and facilitate the organized displacement of poor, disproportionately immigrant people to create space for higher-income classes and real estate speculators (Correia and Wall, 2018: 193–94). On the other hand, they perpetuate racism (Sarbo, 2020: 22). It is the actions of the police that construct areas with a strong immigrant presence, such as hookah bars, as dangerous and are therefore partly responsible for right-wing terrorists choosing them as targets, as was the case in Hanau.[14] Police practices thus disproportionately affect immigrant workers and their German-born children and grandchildren, who are accused of links to organized crime or even involvement in it simply because of their origin.

5 Class, Super-exploitation and the Object of Policing

To comprehend the phenomenon of racist police violence in Germany, it is essential to examine the "relations and activities, of their production, of their intercourse, of their social and political conduct (Marx, 1976: 36)." The current organization of the relations of production must then be brought together with the findings on the fundamental function of the police under capitalism.

Today, it is mainly immigrant labor that works in Germany's low-wage sector. They are super-exploited and generally paid less than their German counterparts. Statistics indicate that in 2019, the risk of poverty among people with

---

minor offenses (possession of narcotics, driving without a license or insulting). See Die LINKE, 2019.

13   This is also illustrated by a look at the selection of so-called crime-ridden locations in Berlin. These are currently Alexanderplatz, Görlitzer Park, Hermannplatz, Hermannstraße, Neukölln S-Bahn station, Kottbusser Tor, Rigaer Straße and Warschauer Straße. Most of these are located in working-class immigrant neighborhoods within the city center. Precarious outer districts in which immigrants live are not on this list.

14   On February 19, 2020, a German racist indiscriminately killed immigrants and deliberately chose hookah bars as crime scenes. See Roldán Mendívil, 2020.

a migration background was more than twice as high as that of people without such a background. Among this former group, foreigners and people who have migrated themselves exhibited an even greater risk of poverty (Bundeszentrale für politische Bildung, 2020).

This also implies a structural change within the most exploited class of wage laborers. In contrast to the 19th and 20th centuries, people with a history of migration now constitute a significant proportion of this group. Historically, the police and criminal justice system have focused on individuals who were at risk of becoming criminals or claiming social benefits due to their particularly high level of poverty. Immigrants are therefore subject to particularly rigorous monitoring, given that they are at an elevated risk of becoming criminals due to their increased poverty. The structural change within the working class therefore makes it necessary to keep a closer watch on the super-exploited immigrant sections of the working class in order to maintain capitalist class relations in Germany today. This follows from the necessity for police work under capitalism to monitor the poor. Therefore, not all immigrants are policed in the same way, as there is no need to police rich immigrants. Nor does it imply that only the immigrant poor are policed. The non-migrant poor are also targeted by the police. However, they are not affected by racism in the form of reified social relations that express the hierarchization of the degree of exploitation in an embodied manner (Darabi et al, 2020).

Today, it is not only the police who control the super-exploited working class. Immigrant workers are also subject to a broad network of social and residence laws. The question of who receives which residence status and who is entitled to which social benefits is part of a mechanism for controlling immigration that follows a capitalist logic of exploitation (Frings, 2017: 172, 181). The threat of possible deportation or the denial of subsistence benefits helps to monitor poor immigrants and push them to the margins of the labor market (Ibid: 174, 181). Welfare state measures establish a disciplinary regime that acts preemptively and threatens sanctions for the slightest infringement (Samour, 2017: 14–15). In this way, the welfare state and the structure of residence and social legislation present a further means of controlling a certain group of people and forcing them into particularly precarious wage labor.

6 Maintaining Exploitation and Super-exploitation

Historically, criminal justice and the police were essential to enforce capitalist relations. It was only with the help of policing that the class of "doubly free" wage laborers was created. Poverty was administered by the police, which involved the criminalization of behaviors which ensured a living without having to work for wages as well as the exclusion of poor foreigners from welfare benefits. At the same time, the police were involved in enforcing the super-exploitation of the colonized and thus in creating a racist division of labor. These are also the basic features of police action today. The reluctance to provide assistance to the foreign poor is evident in contemporary deportation practices and discourses about lazy foreigners who migrate to Germany for the sole purpose of receiving social benefits. In 2010, Thilo Sarrazin argued that "no other immigration [...] is as strongly associated with the use of the welfare state and criminality as Muslim immigration (Sarrazin, 2010)." Furthermore, there is a continued necessity to prevent the impoverished from becoming criminals rather than working for German capital at a low wage. Due to shifts in class composition, this phenomenon is particularly evident among immigrants who live in disproportionate poverty and precariousness. The police and criminal justice system continue to serve as an effective mechanism for maintaining relations of capital.

In the context of demands related to racist police violence, two key points must be considered: firstly, recognizing that police violence, even in its current racist form, is not a flaw in the system, but rather constitutes the system itself. Criticism that calls for greater control of the police on the basis of law fails to address the underlying issue and ignores the fact that the vast authority and discretionary powers of the police, particularly with regard to the use of force, are inherent characteristics of the police in capitalist society (Neocelous, 2021: 194; Correia and Wall, 2018: 182–85). Moreover, it is crucial to recognize that racist police practices are not solely the consequence of individual racist attitudes among police officers. While they undoubtedly represent a pivotal aspect of racist police violence, they are a necessary component of capitalism in order to sustain the racist structures of exploitation within and beyond Germany. The need for German capital to police the lowest strata of the poor persists. The teaching of intercultural skills to police officers, therefore, only scratches the surface of racist incidents and does not address the underlying structural issues that perpetuate racist police violence. A radical critique of the police must understand their role as an instrument of class domination and for maintaining a racist global and domestic division of labor (Marx, 1986: 328–29).

Bibliography

Ackermann, Lutz et al. (2021) Cum-Ex- und Cum-Cum-Geschäfte. 150 Milliarden Euro Schaden, *tagesschau*, Feb. 21, tagesschau.de/investigativ/panorama/cum-ex-cum-cum-101.html.

Amaro Foro e.V. (2020) Geschichte der Rom*nja und Sinti*zze, amaroforo.de/2020/04/26/geschichte-der-roma-und-sinti/.

Autor*innenkollektiv der Berliner Kampagne Ban! (2018) Racial Profiling – Gefährliche Orte abschaffen. In Daniel Loick (ed.), *Kritik der Polizei*. Frankfurt am Main: Campus Verlag.

Becker, Peter (1992) Von ‚Haltlosen' zur ‚Bestie.' Das polizeiliche Bild des ‚Verbrechers' im 19. Jahrhundert. In: Alf Lüdtke (ed.), *‚Sicherheit' und ‚Wohlfahrt.' Polizei, Gesellschaft und Herrschaft im 19. und 20. Jahrhundert*. Frankfurt am Main: suhrkamp.

Belina, Bernd (2018) Wie Polizei Raum und Gesellschaft gestaltet. In: Daniel Loick (ed.), *Kritik der Polizei*. Frankfurt am Main: Campus Verlag.

Blasius, Dirk (1978) *Kriminalität und Alltag. Zur Konfliktgeschichte des Alltagslebens im 19. Jahrhundert*. Göttingen: Vandenhoeck & Ruprecht.

Bonillo, Marion (2001) "Zigeunerpolitik" im Deutschen Kaiserreich 1871–1918. Frankfurt am Main: Peter Lang.

Brazzel, Melanie (2017) Zwei Beispiele für Rassismus und Repression im deutschen Jugendstrafrecht. In: Melanie Brazzel (ed.), *Was macht uns wirklich sicher? Toolkit für Aktivist_innen*, transformativejustice.eu/wp-content/uploads/2018/11/toolkit4-print-1.pdf.

Brettel, Hauke and Hendrik Schneider (2021) *Wirtschaftsstrafrecht*. Baden-Baden: Nomos.

Bundeszentrale für politische Bildung (2020) Armutsgefährdungsquoten von Migranten, *bpb.de*, Nov. 28, bpb.de/nachschlagen/zahlen-und-fakten/soziale-situation-in-deutschland/61788/armut-von-migranten.

Camp, Jordan T. and Christina Heatherton (2016) *Policing the Planet. Why the Policing Crisis Led to Black Lives Matter*. London and New York: Verso.

Correia, David and Tyler Wall (2018) *Police. A Field Guide*. London: Verso.

Darabi, Debora et al. (2020) Polizei ohne Rassismus gibt es nicht, *analyse & kritik*, June 15, akweb.de/ausgaben/661/polizei-ohne-rassismus-gibt-es-nicht/.

Die LINKE (2019). Abgeordnetenhaus Berlin. Schriftliche Anfrage der Abgeordneten Niklas Schrader und Anne Helm (LINKE), *Drucksache 18/20 912: Einsatz gegen »Organisierte Kriminalität« am 27. März 2019 in Berlin-Neukölln (11)*, Sep. 23, pardok.parlament-berlin.de/starweb/adis/citat/VT/18/SchrAnfr/s18-20912.pdf.

El-Tayeb, Fatima and Vanessa E. Thompson (2019) Alltagsrassismus, staatliche Gewalt und koloniale Tradition. Ein Gespräch über Racial Profiling und intersektionale Widerstände in Europa. In: Mohamed Wa Baile et al. (eds.), *Racial Profiling: Struktureller Rassismus und antirassistischer Widerstand*. Bielefeld: Transcript Verlag.

Fings, Karola (2016) *Sinti und Roma. Geschichte einer Minderheit*. München: Verlag C.H. Beck.

Frings, Dorothee (2017) Labor Market Control in the Field of Uncontrolled Migration. In: Moritz Altenried et al. (eds.): *Logistical Borderscapes: Politics and Mediation of Mobile Labor in Germany after the "Summer of Migration."* Münster: Unrast Verlag.

Härter, Karl (2017) *Strafrechts- und Kriminalitätsgeschichte der Frühen Neuzeit.* München and Wien: De Gruyter Oldenbourg.

Jain, Rohit (2019) Von der ‚Zigeunerkartei' zu den ‚Schweizermachern' bis Racial Profiling. In: Mohamed Wa Baile et al. (eds.), *Racial Profiling: Struktureller Rassismus und antirassistischer Widerstand.* Bielefeld: Transcript Verlag.

Jawabreh, Simin (2021) Race Regieren. In: Notausgang: Mapping the Journey of Spaces, *Bärenzwinger Berlin Journal,* baerenzwinger.berlin/Programm/Journal-Notausgang-Mapping-the-Journey-of-Spaces-/.

Kaplan, Debra (2020) *The Patrons and Their Poor. Jewish Community and Public Charity in Early Modern Germany.* Philadelphia: University of Pennsylvania Press.

Kaplan, Debra (2019) The Poor of Your City Come First: Jewish Ritual and the Itinerant Poor in Early Modern Germany. In: David B. Ruderman and Francesca Bregoli (eds.), *Connecting Histories. Jews and Their Others in Early Modern Europe.* Philadelphia: University of Pennsylvania Press.

Liebscher, Doris (2020) Clans statt Rassen – Modernisierungen des Rassismus als Herausforderungen für das Recht, *Kritische Justiz,* vol. 53, no. 4, pp. 529–542, DOI: 10.5771/0023-4834-2020-4-529.

Liebscher, Doris (2021) *Rasse im Recht – Recht gegen Rassismus: Genealogie einer ambivalenten rechtlichen Kategorie.* Berlin: Suhrkamp Verlag.

Marx, Karl (1996) Capital: A Critique of Political Economy, Volume 1. In Karl Marx and Frederick Engels, *Collected Works Vol. 35.* London: Lawrence and Wishart.

Marx, Karl (1987) On the Jewish Question. In: Karl Marx and Frederick Engels, *Collected Works Vol. 3.* London: Lawrence and Wishart.

Marx, Karl (1986) The Civil War in France. In: Karl Marx and Frederick Engels, *Collected Works, Vol. 22.* New York: International Publishers.

Marx, Karl (1976) The German Ideology. In: Karl Marx and Frederick Engels, *Collected Works Vol. 5.* London: Lawrence and Wishart.

Muschalek, Marie (2019) *Violence as Usual: Policing and the Colonial State in German Southwest Africa.* Ithaca, New York: Cornell University Press.

Neocleous, Mark (2021) *A Critical Theory of Police Power: The Fabrication of the Social Order.* London and New York: Verso.

Nitschke, Peter (1990) *Verbrechensbekämpfung und Verwaltung: die Entstehung der Polizei in der Grafschaft Lippe 1700–1814.* Münster and New York: Waxmann.

Pichl, Maximilian (2018) Polizei und Rechtsstaat: Über das Unvermögen, exekutive Gewalt einzuhegen. In: Daniel Loick (ed.), *Kritik der Polizei.* Frankfurt am Main: Campus Verlag.

Pilone, Lea (2021) Frieden für die Obrigkeit, *analyse & kritik*, Apr 20, akweb.de/gesellschaft/die-geschichte-der-polizei-in-europa/.

Rauls, Felix and Thomas Feltes (2021) Clankriminalität. Aktuelle rechtspolitische, kriminologische und rechtliche Probleme, *Neue Kriminalpolitik*, vol. 33, no. 1.

Rodney, Walter (2018) *How Europe Underdeveloped Africa*. London: Verso.

Roldán Mendívil, Eleonora (2020) Das Massaker von Hanau und die Verantwortung des deutschen Staates, *Die Freiheitsliebe*, Feb. 20, diefreiheitsliebe.de/politik/das-massaker-von-hanau-und-die-verantwortung-des-deutschen-staates/.

Rusche, Georg and Otto Kirchheimer (2017) *Punishment and Social Structure*. London and New York: Routledge.

Samour, Nadija (2017) Einleitung: Was ist staatliche Gewalt? In: Melanie Brazzel (ed.), *Was macht uns wirklich sicher? Toolkit für Aktivist_innen*, transformativejustice.eu/wp-content/uploads/2018/11/toolkit4-print-1.pdf.

Sarbo, Bafta (2020) Wie polizeiliches Racial Profiling Rassismus anheizt, *analyse & kritik, Sonderheft Polizeiproblem*, Hamburg.

Sarrazin, Thilo (2010) Bei keiner anderen Religion ist der Übergang zu Gewalt und Terrorismus so fließend, *Bild*, Aug. 26, bild.de/politik/2010/spd-politiker-schreibt-in-seinem-neuen-buch-ueber-den-islam-13749562.bild.html.

Speitkamp, Winfried (2021) *Deutsche Kolonialgeschichte*. Ditzingen: Reclam.

Steinkröger, Julian (2019) *Strafrecht und Strafrechtspflege in den deutschen Kolonien von 1884 bis 1914. Ein Rechtsvergleich innerhalb der Besitzungen des Kaiserreichs in Übersee*. Hamburg: Verlag Dr. Kovac.

Thompson, Vanessa E. (2018) 'There is no justice, there is just us!' Ansätze zu einer postkolonial-feministischen Kritik der Polizei am Beispiel von Racial Profiling. In: Daniel Loick (ed.), *Kritik der Polizei*. Frankfurt am Main: Campus Verlag.

Wacquant, Loïc (2009) *Punishing the Poor: The Neoliberal Government of Social Insecurity*. Durham: Duke University Press.

Weis, Valeria Vegh (2018) *Marxism and Criminology. A History of Criminal Selectivity*. Chicago: Haymarket Books.

ZDF heute (2020) Berliner Landgericht. Goldmünzen-Diebe erhalten mehrjährige Haftstrafen, *ZDF*, Feb. 2, zdf.de/nachrichten/panorama/goldmuenze-raub-bode-museum-100.html.

CHAPTER 7

Beyond the Class Compromise: Racially Segmented Labor Markets in the Context of Intra-EU Migration

Celia Bouali

Racially structured hierarchies are a common feature of labor markets and production structures in capitalist societies.[1] In the course of the coronavirus pandemic, one manifestation of such hierarchies has increasingly become the subject of public debate in Germany: the particular exploitation of Southeast and Eastern European migrants, for example in asparagus fields, meat factories or on large construction sites. Working conditions vary depending on the sector. However, for all sectors, a systemic undercutting of statutory or collectively agreed minimum standards in terms of pay and working conditions are reported.[2]

In discussions surrounding this topic, migrant workers are frequently referred to as "low-wage workers" or "cheap labor." Oftentimes that seems to suggest that the described relations of exploitation are assumed to be inherent to these workers and only arise with their migration to Germany. This attribution is made plausible by the assumption that the workers migrated and entered into these labor relationships "voluntarily." However, the circumstances under which these working conditions arise are thus ignored.

The term "low-wage worker" is associated with a specific relation of exploitation, which is linked to the workers' status as migrants. It can be described as a form of super-exploitation. If we conceptualize the aforementioned minimum

---

1 I would like to thank Manfred Amedick, Luca De Crescenzo, Serhat Karakayalı, Alessandro D'Arcangeli, João Fidalgo, Yunus Aktaş, Fọláṣadé Ajayi, Daniel Weidmann, Christian Frings, Lea Pilone, Henrik Lebuhn and the editors for helpful comments and criticism on the arguments and drafts of this chapter.
2 There are reports of payment below the (sector) minimum wage (or at least below the collectively agreed wage), including non-recognition of qualifications or training periods, wage deductions and unpaid overtime, excessive, hyper-flexible working hours and lack of rest periods, denial of paid leave and paid sick leave, a hazardous and injury-provoking work intensity and a lack of health protection measures, the coupling of housing and workplace and substandard accommodation conditions at exorbitant rents, and sometimes experiences of physical and psychological violence (Molitor, 2015; Jour Fixe, 2020; Lackus and Schell, 2020).

standards as a codification of the value of the commodity of labor-power in the current national class compromise,[3] then falling below those standards implies an exclusion from the class compromise and exploitation beyond the conditions determined therein. Such super-exploitation represents a particular economic and social relation: between migrant workers and capital on the one, and between migrant workers and non-migrant workers on the other hand.

The following text will examine the processes by which migrants from EU countries are turned into "low-wage workers" and the underlying conditions of the relation of exploitation inherent to this designation. Using studies on working conditions in the meat and construction industries, I will examine how different legal frameworks shape the labor market position of EU migrants in Germany, how companies utilize them in their "workforce strategies" and where potential avenues for resistance may be found.[4]

1   Economic Inequalities in the EU as a Context for Migration

The context of intra-EU migration is an EU internal market that is simultaneously interconnected and fragmented. Consequently, migrant workers move between countries with different wage levels and labor and social security systems. Their migration is also embedded in the unequal international division of labor within the EU, which in turn frames their working conditions.

It is often assumed that migrant workers from southern, south-eastern, and eastern Europe exhibit less negative attitudes toward their working conditions and remuneration in Germany than their German counterparts, given the comparatively poorer conditions in their countries of origin, or are more inclined to accept and remain in them (Berntsen, 2016: 480). For the majority of

---

3   Class compromise refers to a structure of political and economic concessions within the framework of the prevailing social mode of production that has emerged in the course of the pacification of class struggles within a country and is secured by the nation state. In addition to compromises in industrial relations, it also includes the level of state regulation during a historical period.

4   In this article, I focus on intra-EU migration, since a large proportion of the workers in the relations of exploitation under investigation come from within the EU and specific legal frameworks play a role here. However, since many workers without EU citizenship also work under similar conditions in the sectors under consideration, it is equally necessary to examine the connections between different migration regimes and the associated processes of working class recomposition, albeit this can only be hinted at here. Due to the date of first publication of the original text, more recent developments regarding the relevant legal frameworks and industry structures could not be covered here.

workers, the decision to work in Germany is in fact based on economic considerations: A precarious starting position in the country of origin and the higher wages in Germany make migration an opportunity to overcome financial difficulties, offer the family a better standard of living or finance a lifetime project such as home ownership (Wagner, 2015a: 700; Thörnqvist and Bernhardsson, 2014: 23–36; Voivozeanu, 2019: 92–93). Particularly in the case of individuals who repeatedly enter into such labor relationships for a limited period of time, with the center of their lives remaining in their country of origin, it is plausible that the wages they receive are more likely to be measured against the cost of living in that country.[5]

However, this *dual frame of reference* (Waldinger and Lichter, 2019; Piore, 1979) does not refer to a "habitual satisfaction" with poorer conditions, but rather to the socio-economic parameters of labor mobility. Employment is taken up in the context of a more or less precarious starting position, which, in addition to the frame of reference, also shapes the conditions for seeking and taking up employment. For example, researchers have observed that the range of resources available to workers when seeking employment affects the duration of their search for (potentially more advantageous) positions (Felbo-Kolding et al, 2019).

2   Shaping EU Migrant Labor within the Legal Framework

The labor relationships of EU migrants are also embedded in a framework of EU and national legislation. In contrast to "third-country nationals," EU citizens do not require a residence permit or work permit to work in another EU country.[6] Nevertheless, their migration takes place under certain legal parameters, which have implications for their working and living conditions. The regulation of EU-internal labor mobility distinguishes between different forms of mobility: the posting of workers, which is derived from the freedom to provide services, and the free movement of persons, which is granted by EU

---

5 It is important to note that "mobile workers" do not necessarily stay "mobile workers." Not only do migration projects change, the character of labor relationships and forms of mobility influence one another. Particularly precarious working conditions may, for instance, make it difficult to relocate to Germany, or relocating may change how working conditions and pay are perceived. How mobility is organized is therefore an important factor for the organization of labor relationships.
6 However, there were exceptions during the transition period following the EU's eastward expansion (Dälken, 2012: 9–10).

citizenship (and the freedom of movement for workers and freedom of establishment contained therein).

3 Mobility of Labor under the Posting of Workers Directive

EU-based companies are entitled to offer their services throughout the entire territory of the Union and to post their employees to another EU country for a limited period of time so that they can carry out their work on behalf of the company. The posted employees are generally subject to the labor and social security law of the posting country (with time restrictions). However, several labor law provisions of the host country must be complied with (Kennedy, 2024).

Such posted work relationships are prevalent in certain sectors, such as construction, and have been the subject of extensive research. The studies demonstrated that the legal framework for the posting of workers that emerged between the 1980s and 2000s had undermined the principle of territoriality by introducing exceptions to national labor law. Consequently, German labor law did not necessarily apply to workers on construction sites in Germany. This made it easier to circumvent labor law provisions and, in effect, "deregulated" the employment relationships of posted workers (Seikel, 2020; Arnholtz and Lillie, 2020: 4).

It is true that the legal framework has changed in recent years, with some of the earlier points of criticism now being addressed (Seikel, 2020: 6–9). Nevertheless, it remains the case that in the initial 12 to 18 months of the posting, the employment relationships of posted workers are at least partially exempt from the national labor law framework of the country in which the work is performed and are located in a kind of special legal zone between the legal frameworks of the posting and the host country (Wagner, 2015b: 1373; Arnholtz and Lillie, 2020: 8). Against the backdrop of the major socio-economic and regulatory differences within the EU, posted workers may be placed at a disadvantage with regard to social security and labor law, which translates to a reduction in wage costs for companies.

Furthermore, the monitoring and enforcement of labor law provisions is more challenging within this legal framework. The transnational nature of employment relationships can make it difficult to ascertain whether an employment relationship is a "genuine" or a sham posting and whether the provisions that nevertheless apply are complied with in the event of actual postings (Wagner, 2015b: 1376–78; Cremers, 2020: 128–46).

The interplay of all these factors allows companies to utilize postings as a means of *regime shopping* between different national legal frameworks or to circumvent labor law provisions altogether.[7]

4 Mobility of Labor within the Free Movement of Persons Framework

It should be noted that by far not all EU migrant workers are posted workers. Many are in Germany within the framework of the free movement of persons. As EU citizens, they have the right to move and reside freely within the territory of the EU and to pursue paid employment or run a business in other member states while being treated equally to citizens of these states (Marzocchi, 2023). Their employment relationships are governed by the labor and social security law of the country in which they are employed.

In the period following the EU's eastward expansion, however, this right to freedom of movement for the "new" EU citizens was initially constrained in Germany (and other "old member states") through the implementation of so-called transitional regulations. As a result, those affected were compelled to pursue other forms of labor mobility that were associated with less protection under labor law and more precarious employment, such as posting or seasonal work (Wagner and Hassel, 2017: 418).

Moreover, even beyond the transitional arrangements, the right to free movement enshrined in the European treaties is increasingly subject to conditions and restrictions (Voigt, 2017: 9).[8] For instance, the Free Movement Directive 2004/38/EC stipulates that EU citizens residing in other member states for a period exceeding three months must either be gainfully employed or "have sufficient resources for themselves and their family members not to become a burden on the social assistance system of the host Member State during their period of residence and have comprehensive sickness insurance cover in the host Member State (Marzocchi, 2023)."[9]

This "economic qualification" of the right to freedom of movement was expanded in the context of racist debates about "social tourism" to restrict the

---

7 Nathan Lillie (2010: 683–704) has pointed out parallels between offshoring and posting, arguing that the latter can function as a form of legal offshoring for industries such as construction where it is not possible to relocate production for cost reduction.
8 More recent developments, which partly deviate from this trend, could not be included in the analysis due to the date of first publication of the original text.
9 However, there is the possibility of acquiring permanent residence (without requirements) after five years (§ 16(1), § 21 RL 2004/38/EG).

social rights of EU migrants. In several rulings since 2014, the Court of Justice of the European Union (CJEU) has declared national (primarily German) law that restricts EU citizens' access to social benefits to be in accordance with EU law and thus confirmed it.[10] The verdicts argue that the social rights of EU citizens are subject to legal residence requirements, which in turn are linked to economic preconditions. Consequently, de facto access to the right to freedom of movement or to full EU citizenship rights is contingent on certain economic conditions (Kötter, 2016: 3–4; Riedner, 2017: 18). Only "economically active" EU citizens are included in the social security system, while those who are not employed or are seeking employment may "lose their social rights and [...] following an individual assessment, may also lose their freedom of movement and can even be deported (Riedner, 2015: 18)."[11]

The limited social substance of EU citizenship and the linking of the right to free movement to "economic activity" (or financial autonomy) reveals an economization of citizenship and a precarization of citizenship rights. This is consistent with a logic of productivity in the regulation of mobility within the EU. The objective is to control or "manage" migration in order to enhance its economic utility, to sanction "unproductivity," and to discipline EU migrants into (precarious) wage labor (Ibid).

In her case study of Munich, Lisa Riedner provides an analysis of the administrative practice that implements this logic. She elucidates how social welfare authorities utilize requests for social benefits from EU migrants as an opportunity to ascertain their right of residence, thereby becoming a kind of border authority that endeavors to prevent "unwanted" migration. Concurrently, the foreigners' office acts as "a labor activation agency (Ibid)." It sends letters to

---

10   In the case of Elisabeta Dano and her son, the CJEU ruled that the exclusion of "economically inactive" EU citizens without sufficient resources from access to "special non-contributory social benefits" does not contradict EU legislation, as they do not enjoy a right of residence in the host member state in accordance with Directive 2004/38/EC (C-333/13 Jobcenter Leipzig v. Dano, ECLI:EU:C:2014:2358). In the case of Nazifě Alimanovič and her family, the possibility of exclusion was extended to EU citizens residing in another member state solely for the purpose of seeking employment (C-67/14 Jobcenter Berlin Neukölln v. Alimanovič, ECLI:EU:C:2015:597). In the case of Jovanna García-Nieto and her family, the court ruled that economically inactive EU citizens can also be excluded from access to "special non-contributory social benefits" for the first three months of their stay in another member state (C-299/14 Jobcenter Kreis Recklinghausen v. García-Nieto and Others, ECLI:EU:C:2016:114). More recent rulings, which partly deviate from this trend, could not be included in the analysis due to the date of first publication of the original text.

11   More recent rulings, which partly deviate from the trend described above, could not be included in the analysis due to the date of first publication of the original text.

EU citizens who have applied for social benefits, threatening them with the loss of their residence permit or deportation.[12] "In terms of immigration law, it is not 'worthwhile' to initiate the deportation, as the people affected could re-enter the country immediately," explains a manager at the foreigners' office. According to him, "his agency does not seek to deport people, but to integrate them. The aim is to ensure that those affected look for work (Riedner, 2017: 104)." Riedner asserts that this strategy of forcing EU migrants into further wage labor is often effective (Ibid: 103).

Consequently, some researchers link EU "migration management" to *workfare* programs[13] and a general tendency of precarization of work. Gabriella Alberti (2017, as cited in Alberti, 2015) argues:

> These processes appear instrumental to the 'government of mobility' in Europe [...] making migrants more available, disposable, and compliant vis-a-vis their employers. It is the reproduction of a precarious workforce, with no social security cushion, under constant risk of falling into poverty, and pushed to accept lower standards that such regulatory restrictions concur to generate.

5   EU Migration Regimes: Structuring Precarious Labor Relationships

The described regulatory framework for European internal mobility creates conditions that render EU-migrant workers more vulnerable and precarious than their counterparts from the respective countries. Despite formally having the same rights as nationals of the respective country, these workers are more likely to enter into labor relationships in which minimum standards are undercut. The specific migrant statuses of workers structure their access to the labor market, shape their position in terms of labor and social law, and thus influence the conditions under which they sell their labor-power as well as their relations to the capitalists opposite to them.

---

12   In some cases, this is done without legal permission. In one case reported by Riedner, the benefits received were top-up benefits. As the people concerned had EU employee status, the receipt of social benefits alone should not have had a negative impact on their right of residence. They nevertheless received the letter.

13   This primarily refers to the social and labor market policy programs introduced in various countries since the 1990s, which link social benefits to an obligation to (take up) gainful employment, usually in combination with an expansion of the low-wage sector and the flexibilization of gainful employment.

Bridget Anderson points out that migration regimes produce different forms of migrant labor and make them available for certain labor relationships: "In practice rather than a tap regulating entry, immigration controls might be more usefully conceived as constructing certain types of workers, and facilitating certain types of employment relations, many of which are particularly suited to precarious work (Anderson, 2007: 2)." The "low-wage worker" is thus, among other things, a product of the intra-EU migration regime.

The legal position of EU migrant workers in relation to other migrants can be theorized by drawing on the concept of *differential inclusion*. This refers to an increasing multiplication of migration statuses and interwoven social positions (Mezzadra and Neilson, 2013) or "the link between migration control and regimes of labour management that create different degrees of precarity, vulnerability and freedom by granting and closing access to resources and rights according to economic, individualizing, and racist rationales (Casas-Cortes et al, 2014: 79)." Intra-EU migration regimes produce ever more differentiations regarding both migrations within the EU and from outside the Union, which is why Rutvica Andrijasevic and others call for the connections between intra-EU and other migration to be highlighted. A blanket distinction between intra-EU "mobility" and "migration" from "third countries" not only draws on problematic discursive figures that naturalize the results of migration regimes. A separate analysis also misses the similarities in the living realities and working conditions of migrants with different statuses, the interplay of different migration regimes[14] and the associated dynamics of working class recomposition in the EU (Andrijasevic et al, 2016).

The establishment of EU citizenship was accompanied by a reinforcement of the hierarchy between EU citizens and "third-country nationals," a phenomenon that Étienne Balibar has described as "European apartheid (Balibar, 2003: 172)." At the same time, hierarchies between member states have been renewed and intensified (Nicolaus, 2014: 114). This has led to an (analogous) multiplication of statuses within European citizenship. In the wake of the 2007/2008 financial crisis and subsequent European austerity policy, existing economic and political disparities between Southern and Northern, as well as Eastern and Western EU member states have increased (Ibid: 114–15). The regulation of labor mobility within the EU is linked to these inequalities and the interwoven racist debates, which translate into precarious labor market positions for certain EU migrants.

---

14 For example, Bosnian and Serbian workers are often posted from Slovenia to work on construction sites in Germany.

6 Sector-Specific "Workforce Strategies" – Construction Industry and Meat Industry

The concrete organization of their labor relationships is the result of a specific entrepreneurial practice that has developed in response to the legal provisions on labor mobility and economic inequalities, as well as the specific industry structures.

This can be illustrated by the construction industry. In light of the significant role of labor costs and high flexibility requirements in construction production, as well as a production structure in which many small companies vie for contracts in a subcontractor chain dominated by a few large contractors (Fellini et al, 2007: 281; Eccles, 1981), "cheap labor" has emerged as a pivotal element in the business model of construction companies.

Large construction contracts usually work according to the following pattern:

> Large construction sites are usually structured in the form of a pyramid. At the top is the developer [...]. Developers bear the legal and economic responsibility for the construction. The next level down is the general contractor, which is responsible for planning and providing the construction services for the entire project. One level further down the pyramid, it commissions various subcontractors to provide the construction services, who in turn regularly pass on certain tasks to other subcontractors, yet another level below. At the lowest level, as flexible a labor force as possible is hired.
> LACKUS AND SCHELL, 2020: 143

The companies employ a variety of "workforce strategies (Nienhüser, 1999)." These strategies involve a range of recruitment, employment, and deployment methods, which are embedded in distinct regulatory frameworks. They create different statuses for workers, which are associated with varying legal entitlements.

In addition to the aforementioned use of labor in the form of posted workers, it is also possible to employ migrants at a German subcontractor. In this case, EU citizens are integrated into the production structure within the framework of the free movement of workers via their contract of employment with the subcontractor and its service contract[15] with the company above them (Lackus

---

15 With a few exceptions, temporary agency work is prohibited in the German construction industry, so these companies usually act as construction companies fulfilling a service contract.

and Schell, 2020: 144). Although these workers are employed under German labor law and are subject to social security contributions, reports and research on such labor relationships in the construction and meat industries show that minimum standards on pay and working conditions are often undercut in these arrangements as well (Birke and Bluhm, 2019). Another "workforce strategy" is the use of "self-employed workers" in the context of freedom of establishment, which often merely constitutes dependent employment in disguise. Self-employed workers do not possess employee status and "work without basic employee rights such as protection against dismissal, sick leave, and regulation of working hours (Lackus and Schell, 2020: 144)." Finally, construction companies also resort entirely to irregular employment. For those affected, "labor law standards […] are effectively suspended and access to social security benefits is also limited based on this form of employment (Ibid)."

In these "workforce strategies," the various forms of intra-EU mobility regulation, broader labor and corporate law frameworks, the choice and practical form of the employment relationship and its incorporation into the production structure are all intertwined. Together, these factors produce labor relationships in which the super-exploitation of migrant workers occurs.

7   Mediation Infrastructure

In addition to these "workforce strategies," the organization of labor relationships is also embedded in a mediation infrastructure[16] that encompasses the recruitment of workers and their integration into production structures, the handling of their travel to the workplace and the organization of their accommodation. It makes migrant labor available for exploitation under specific conditions and also isolates, controls and disciplines it.

Mediation infrastructures shape the spatial and temporal dimensions of labor mobility, making access to labor more flexible, while also situating it in different socio-economic contexts at the same time: short-notice and short-term placements, for example, are geared towards maintaining circular forms of migration where migrants move without relocating (Schling, 2022: 301–16). The dynamic described above, through which lower reproduction costs elsewhere in the EU become the benchmark for wage levels, only becomes utilizable in this way.

---

16   Cf. the concept of migration infrastructure in Xiang and Lindquist, 2014.

Mediation, understood as "the organization of the 'encounter' between capital and labour (Mezzadra, 2016: 39)," is increasingly being viewed in research on migrant labor as a separate field of economic activity that needs to be understood in the context of "migration management" and the flexibilization of labor markets (Ibid; Gammeltoft-Hansen and Sørensen, 2013).

Mediation and production structures are closely interwoven. Creating the organizational conditions for the specific exploitation of migrant labor involves everything from placing workers and organizing their integration into production to "activating" and disciplining them in production itself. The various aspects are closely intertwined: for example, linking employment and accommodation can create additional dependencies. The constant threat of losing one's employment and thus also one's accommodation can be used to intensify work and extend working hours. The form of mediation thus contributes directly to the commanding power of capital within the production process. Furthermore, arbitrary deductions for board and lodging reduce the actual hourly wage that is paid.

8 Power Resources of Migrant Labor

Against this backdrop, migrant workers in the German meat industry, for instance, can quickly appear as an easily replaceable workforce that companies can freely dispose of. In fact, turnover is often part of the business model of companies, which use transfers and dismissals to exert pressure on workers and the constant recomposition of the workforce as an instrument of disorganization (Birke and Bluhm, 2020: 504; Birke, 2021: 36–39).

However, the "workforce strategies" of companies and the mechanisms of making labor available are "problem-prone" and workers are not powerless. Even if the jobs of migrant workers are often labeled as "unskilled," they still require training and practice, and semi-skilled workers in certain areas cannot simply be replaced (Birke and Bluhm, 2019: 29).[17] Strategies that are designed to make labor "available" in the most flexible and cost-effective manner thus run counter to an interest emerging from the logic of production: the interest in a stable workforce trained according to production requirements (Birke and Bluhm, 2019: 30–31). Workers are well aware of their *marketplace bargaining power* and *workplace bargaining power* (Silver, 2003: 13; Wright, 2000: 962), as

---

17 Beyond the issue of designating jobs as "skilled" or "unskilled," the problem of (non-)recognition of professional qualifications also plays a role for the position of workers (Birke and Bluhm, 2020: 503).

is demonstrated by mobility practices and collective actions in the workplace (Birke and Bluhm, 2020: 504).

This is because labor mobility does not simply follow the described "migration management" or entrepreneurial "workforce strategies." In proposing the concept of an *autonomy of migration* (Bojadžijev and Karakayalı, 2007: 209–15), researchers point out that it is linked to the will, interests and hopes of the bearers of that labor-power who pursue their life plans as they engage with prevailing social conditions (Ibid: 213–14; Karakayalı and Tsianos, 2007: 16).

Migration can thus be understood, for example, as an "exit strategy (Hirschmann, 1970)" by which workers escape the even more intensive relations of exploitation in their country of origin, which in turn has an impact on labor and power relations there. Guglielmo Meardi notes that the significant "exit" of workers from the "new member states" following the EU's eastward expansion has compelled companies and governments in those countries to make concessions regarding wage levels and employment conditions and also contributed to a partial revitalization of trade unions (Meardi, 2012: 105).

Birke and Bluhm point out that mobility can also be a power resource for migrants with regard to working conditions in the German meat industry. The threat of workers leaving the company and the actual implementation of such "exit strategies" (which involve both changing companies and industries, and moving to take up work in England, Denmark or the Netherlands) is increasingly becoming a problem for meat companies and forces them into concessions (Birke and Bluhm, 2019: 34–39).[18]

However, the availability of such exit options is contingent upon legal and economic parameters. As demonstrated by Birke and Bluhm, the capacity to exercise mobility as a power resource is not equally accessible to all workers. Factors such as residence status, legal entitlements that facilitate exit options like access to social benefits, varying production and market power resulting from the division of labor in production, and mobility-related factors such as age and family status all impinge upon individual workers' possibilities to "exit" labor relationships (Ibid: 34–35; Birke, 2021: 38).

Moreover, the aforementioned exit points are not a given. Comparatively better working conditions in the Danish meat industry are at least partly due to a high level of unionization (Wagner and Refslund, 2016). Industrial power relations may, however, be subject to change under pressure of competition

---

18 Due to the date of first publication of the original text, more recent developments in the industry following the introduction of the Arbeitsschutzkontrollgesetz ("Labor Protection Control Act") are not covered here.

with the German production model and the associated conditions, as is evidenced by the relocation of production to Germany (Bernhold, 2020).[19]

9 Organizing and Resistance in the Workplace and Beyond

As individual exit strategies are inherently limited in their ability to address the underlying conditions, the necessity for collective organizing becomes evident. Many studies emphasize that workers' individual strategies may stabilize prevailing conditions and that the resistance options of those affected are limited (Berntsen, 2016). In his research on the meat industry, however, Birke points out that workers' struggles do take place – albeit mostly "under the radar" of German trade unions and beyond media attention (Birke, 2021: 35).

An exemplary exception was the struggle of workers hired for the construction of the *Mall of Berlin*. When they were robbed of their wages, the workers initiated a protracted labor struggle in 2014 that attracted national attention and resulted in the building being dubbed "Mall of Shame." On the one hand, their struggle demonstrated the potential for collective action; on the other hand, it revealed the limitations of such action within the context of the prevailing structural conditions. It led to a series of legal proceedings against the responsible subcontractors and the general contractor, which the workers ultimately won. However, the convicted companies were able to avoid responsibility by filing for bankruptcy, so that the "acquired legal titles could not be redeemed and the workers' pockets remained empty (Lackus and Schell, 2020: 10)." When lawsuits filed against the mall's investor proved unsuccessful, the legal route was exhausted. By this time, the majority of the workers, whose livelihoods had been threatened by wage theft and some of whom had been evicted from their employment-related accommodation in the course of the conflict, had already left Berlin and sought work elsewhere (Ibid: 11).

This and other examples demonstrate that the struggles do not "only" concern the situation in the workplace, but the entire framework conditions that give rise to the relations of exploitation. Resistance to racist debates on intra-EU migration, in which Romani people are particularly attacked, and the associated laws and administrative practices as well as demands for improved working conditions, access to social security systems and adequate housing are intertwined. This is because the conditions addressed are simultaneously

---

19 Due to the date of first publication of the original text, more recent developments in the industry following the introduction of the Arbeitsschutzkontrollgesetz ("Labor Protection Control Act") are not covered here.

relevant to the biographies of individual workers and shape their position as workers (Birke and Bluhm, 2020: 503–04).

10 Beyond National Class Compromises

The labor relationships of EU migrants are shaped by the interplay of several factors:
- The specific legal framing of labor relationships; here, migration policies specifically concerning migrant workers as well as general labor market and social policies intertwine and produce a workfarist and precarizing "migration management." This interplay is accompanied by racist debates about "low-wage workers" and "social tourism."
- Industry-specific production models and the associated mediation infrastructures with and in which migrant labor is made available and disciplined.
- Workers' practices and struggles in all these areas (embedded in the broader structures and dynamics of class struggle).

The specific relations of exploitation of migrant workers contain the contradictions of the unequal international division of labor and bring to light the exclusions inherent in the national class compromise.[20] Social democratic concepts of mediation, which are committed to this class compromise therefore prove to be an inappropriate response to these forms of exploitation.

This is evident not least in the ambivalent role of trade union strategies based on social partnership, and that of labor control authorities. The former have worked to secure the boundaries of the national class compromise. Trade union support for the transitional arrangements and the resulting segmented industrial relations partly reinforced the disadvantaged position of migrants, for instance (Wagner and Refslund, 2016; Wagner and Hassel, 2017: 411). In debates on the labor relationships considered here, labor control authorities are regularly presented as a solution. However, calls for more controls often neglect the question of who actually benefits from them. Apart from difficulties in providing evidence and sanctioning violations, controls often do not work in the workers' favor. This is partly due to the fact that they are not necessarily geared towards enforcing the labor rights of those affected. For example, "the FKS [Finanzkontrolle Schwarzarbeit of the German customs authorities] only claims the social security contributions that are due, while the workers

---

20 Cf. Étienne Balibar's concept of "national-social state" in Balibar, 2014: 147; Cf. also Riedner, 2018: 316–18.

have to assert their rights individually (Bosch et al, 2018: 5)." Furthermore, reports have emerged of raids in the meat industry, during which workers from "third countries" have faced the harshest consequences. This is because sanctions were imposed on "perpetrators and victims alike, meaning that those who are exploited particularly brazenly are potentially being deported. Those who exploit particularly brazenly, on the other hand, are only prosecuted to the extent that they are directly guilty of 'smuggling,' while the companies supplied with fresh labor can wash their hands of it (Birke, 2021: 31)."

There are increasing efforts by trade unions and other institutions to advocate for the interests of migrant workers. However, a response to their superexploitation ultimately requires a militant and transnational class standpoint that goes beyond national class compromises.

Bibliography

Alberti, Gabriella (2015) Connessioni Precarie: The Government of Mobility 2, The (United) Kingdom of Workfare versus Welfare for Migrants, Part 1, *Connessioni Precarie*, connessioniprecarie.org/2015/01/24/the-government-of-mobility-2-the-united-kingdom-of-workfare-versus-welfare-for-migrants/.

Alberti, Gabriella (2017) The Government of Migration Through Workfare in the UK. Towards a Shrinking Space of Mobility and Social Rights? *movements. Journal für kritische Migrations- und Grenzregimeforschung*, vol. 3, no. 1, movements-journal.org/issues/04.bewegungen/08.alberti--government-migration-workfare-uk-mobility-social-rights.pdf.

Anderson, Bridget (2007) Battles in Time. The Relation between Global and Labour Mobilities, *University of Oxford, Centre on Migration, Policy and Society*, working paper no. 55, compas.ox.ac.uk/wp-content/uploads/WP-2007-055-Anderson_Global_Labour_Mobilities.pdf.

Andrijasevic, Rutvica et al. (2016) Introduzione. Le migrazioni lavorative intra-UE, modelli, pratiche e traiettorie di mobilità dei cittadini europei, *Mondi Migranti*, special issue no. 3, pp. 24–27, DOI: 10.3280/MM2016-003002.

Arnholtz, Jens and Nathan Lillie (2020) European Integration and the Reconfiguration of National Industrial Relations. Posted Work as a Driver of Institutional Change. In: Arnholtz and Lillie (eds.), *Posted Work in the European Union. The Political Economy of Free Movement*. New York: Routledge.

Balibar, Étienne (2014) Communism and Citizenship: On Nicos Poulantzas. In: Étienne Balibar, *Equaliberty*. Durham and London: Duke University Press.

Balibar, Étienne (2003) *We, the people of Europe? Reflections on Transnational Citizenship*. Princeton: Princeton University Press.

Bernhold, Christin (2020) Die Fleischindustrie. Ein Brennglas-Effekt auf Probleme der kapitalistischen Produktionsweise, *isw München*, isw-muenchen.de/online-publikationen/texte-artikel/3443-42die-fleischindustrie-ein-brennglas-effekt-auf-probleme-der-kapitalistischen-produktionsweise.

Berntsen, Lisa (2016) Reworking labour practices: on the agency of unorganized mobile migrant construction workers, *Work, Employment and Society*, vol. 30, no. 3.

Birke, Peter and Felix Bluhm (2019) Arbeitskräfte willkommen. Neue Migration zwischen Grenzregime und Erwerbsarbeit,"*Sozial.Geschichte Online*, vol. 25, pp. 11–43.

Birke, Peter and Felix Bluhm (2020) Der Skandal und die Folgen. Perspektiven der Abschaffung von Werkverträgen und Leiharbeit in der Fleischindustrie, *WSI Mitteilungen*, vol. 73, no. 6.

Birke, Peter (2021) Die Fleischindustrie in der Coronakrise. Eine Studie zu Migration, Arbeit und multipler Prekarität, *Sozial.Geschichte Online*, vol. 29.

Bojadžijev, Manuela and Serhat Karakayalı (2007) Autonomie der Migration. 10 Thesen zu einer Methode. In: Forschungsgruppe TRANSIT MIGRATION (eds.), *Turbulente Ränder: Neue Perspektiven auf Migration an den Grenzen Europas, Kultur und soziale Praxis*. Bielefeld: transcript Verlag.

Bosch, Gerhard et al. (2018) Kontrolle und Durchsetzung von Mindestarbeitsbedingungen. Einhaltung von Mindestlohnansprüchen am Beispiel des Bauhauptgewerbes, der Fleischwirtschaft und des Gastgewerbes, *Hans Böckler Stiftung: Working Paper Forschungsförderung*, vol. 095.

Casas-Cortes, Maribel et al. (2014) New Keywords. Migration and Borders, *Cultural Studies*, vol. 29, no. 1, pp. 55–87, DOI: 10.1080/09502386.2014.891630.

Cremers, Jan (2020) Market Integration, Cross-Border Recruitment, and Enforcement of Labour Standards. A Dutch Case. In: Jens Arnholtz and Nathan Lillie (eds.), *Posted Work in the European Union. The Political Economy of Free Movement*. New York: Routledge.

Dälken, Michaela (2012) *Grenzenlos faire Mobilität? Zur Situation von mobilen Beschäftigten aus den mittel- und osteuropäischen Staaten*. Berlin: Projekt Faire Mobilität des DGB-Bundesvorstandes.

Eccles, Robert G. (1981) The quasifirm in the construction industry, *Journal of Economic Behavior & Organization*, vol. 2, no. 4, pp. 335–57.

Felbo-Kolding, Jonas et al. (2019) A Division of Labour? Labour Market Segmentation by Region of Origin: The Case of Intra-EU Migrants in the UK, Germany and Denmark, *Journal of Ethnic and Migration Studies*, vol. 45, no. 15, pp. 2820–43, DOI: 10.1080/1369183X.2018.1518709.

Fellini, Ivana et al. (2007) Recruitment processes and labour mobility: the construction industry in Europe, *Work, Employment and Society*, vol. 21, no. 2.

Gammeltoft-Hansen, Thomas and Ninna Nyberg Sørensen (2013) *The Migration Industry and the Commercialization of International Migration*. London and New York: Routledge.

Hirschman, Albert O. (1970) *Exit, Voice, and Loyalty. Responses to Decline in Firms, Organizations, and States*. Cambridge: Harvard University Press.

Jour Fixe Gewerkschaftslinke Hamburg (2020) Das "System Tönnies" – organisierte Kriminalität und moderne Sklaverei. Aufhebung der Werkverträge und des Subunternehmertums! Hamburg: Die Buchmacherei.

Karakayalı, Serhat and Vassilis Tsianos (2007) Movements That Matter. Eine Einleitung. In: Forschungsgruppe TRANSIT MIGRATION (eds.), *Turbulente Ränder*. Bielefeld: transcript Verlag.

Kennedy, Aoife (2024) Posting of Workers, *EU Parliament*, europarl.europa.eu /factsheets/en/sheet/37/posting-of-workers.

Kötter, Ute (2016) Die Entscheidung des EuGH in der Rechtssache Alimanović. Das Ende der europäischen Sozialbürgerschaft? *info also*, no. 1.

Lackus, Hendrik and Olga Schell (2020) *Mall of Shame. Kampf um Würde und Lohn*. Berlin: Die Buchmacherei.

Lillie, Nathan (2010) Bringing the Offshore Ashore. Transnational Production, Industrial Relations and the Reconfiguration of Sovereignty, *International Studies Quarterly*, vol. 54, no. 3, pp. 683–704.

Marzocchi, Ottavio (2023) Free Movement of Persons. *EU Parliament*, europarl.europa. eu/factsheets/en/sheet/147/free-movement-of-persons.

Meardi, Guglielmo (2012) Union Immobility? Trade Unions and the Freedoms of Movement in the Enlarged EU, *British Journal of Industrial Relations*, vol. 50, no. 1.

Mezzadra, Sandro and Brett Neilson (2013) *Border as Method, or, the Multiplication of Labor*. Durham and London: Duke University Press.

Mezzadra, Sandro (2016) MLC 2015 Keynote: What's at Stake in the Mobility of Labour? Borders, Migration, Contemporary Capitalism, *Migration, Mobility & Displacement*, vol. 2, no. 1.

Molitor, Carmen (2015) Geschäftsmodell Ausbeutung. Wenn europäische Arbeitnehmer _innen in Deutschland um ihre Rechte betrogen werden, Friedrich Ebert Stiftung, Berlin, library.fes.de/pdf-files/id/11307.pdf.

Nicolaus, Noel David (2014) Zwischen citizenship und commoning. Recht auf Stadt in Zeiten der Eurokrise, *sub\urban. zeitschrift für kritische stadtforschung*, vol. 2, no. 3.

Nienhüser, Werner (1999) "Legal, illegal, ... " – Die Nutzung und Ausgestaltung von Arbeitskräftestrategien in der Bauwirtschaft, *Industrielle Beziehungen/The German Journal of Industrial Relations*, vol. 3, pp. 292–319.

Piore, Michael J. (1979) *Birds of passage. Migrant labor and industrial societies*. Cambridge: Cambridge University Press.

Riedner, Lisa (2015) Justice for Janitors? Marktbürgerschaft, Freizügigkeit und EU-Migrantinnen im Arbeitskampf. Einblicke in ein aktivistisches Forschungsprojekt, *movements. Journal für kritische Migrations- und Grenzregimeforschung*, vol. 1, no. 2.

Riedner, Lisa (2017) Aktivierung durch Ausschluss. Sozial- und migrationspolitische Transformationen unter den Bedingungen der EU-Freizügigkeit, *movements. Journal für kritische Migrations- und Grenzregimeforschung*, vol. 3, no. 1.

Riedner, Lisa (2018) *Arbeit! Wohnen! Urbane Auseinandersetzungen um EU-Migration. Eine Untersuchung zwischen Wissenschaft und Aktivismus*. Münster. edition assemblage.

Schling, Hannah (2022) 'Just-in-time' migrant workers in Czechia: racialisation and dormitory labour regimes. In: Elena Baglioni et al. (eds.), *Labour Regimes and Global Production*. Newcastle: Agenda Publishing.

Seikel, Daniel (2020) Die Revision der Entsenderichtlinie. Wie der lange Kampf um die Wiedereinbettung exterritorialisierten Arbeitsrechtes gewonnen wurde, *WSI Working Paper*, no. 212.

Silver, Beverly J. (2003) *Forces of Labor. Workers' Movements and Globalization since 1870*. Cambridge: Cambridge University Press.

Thörnqvist, Christer and Sebastian Bernhardsson (2014) Their own stories – how Polish construction workers posted to Sweden experience their job situation, or resistance versus life projects, *Transfer: European Review of Labour and Research*, vol. 21, no. 1, pp. 23–36, DOI: 10.1177/1024258914561409.

Voigt, Claudius (2017) *Ausgeschlossen oder privilegiert? Zur aufenthalts- und sozialrechtlichen Situation von Unionsbürgern und ihren Familienangehörigen*. Berlin: Der Paritätische Gesamtverband.

Voivozeanu, Alexandra (2019) Precarious Posted Migration. The Case of Romanian Construction and Meat-Industry Workers in Germany, *Central and Eastern European Migration Review*, vol. 85, no. 2, pp. 85–99, DOI: 10.17467/ceemr.2019.07.

Wagner, Bettina and Anke Hassel (2017) Arbeitsmigration oder Auswanderung? Eine Analyse atypischer Arbeitsmigration nach Deutschland, *WSI Mitteilungen*, vol. 6.

Wagner, Ines and Bjarke Refslund (2016) Understanding the diverging trajectories of slaughterhouse work in Denmark and Germany: A power resource approach, *European Journal of Industrial Relations*, vol. 22, no. 4, pp. 335–51.

Wagner, Ines (2015a) Rule Enactment in a Pan-European Labour Market: Transnational Posted Work in the German Construction Sector," *British Journal of Industrial Relations*, vol. 53, no. 4, pp. 692–710.

Wagner, Ines (2015b) The Political Economy of Borders in a 'Borderless' European Labour Market, *Journal of Common Market Studies*, vol. 53, no. 6, pp. 1370–85.

Waldinger, Roger and Michael I. Lichter (2019) *How the Other Half Works. Immigration and the Social Organization of Labor*. Berkeley: University of California Press.

Wright, Erik Olin (2000) Working-Class Power, Capitalist-Class Interests, and Class Compromise, *American Journal of Sociology*, vol. 105, no. 4.

Xiang, Biao and Johan Lindquist (2014) Migration Infrastructure, *International Migration Review*, vol. 48, no. 1, pp. 122–48.

CHAPTER 8

The Right-Wing Project and the Crisis of Capitalism: A Materialist Analysis of the Rise of the Right in Germany

Sebastian Friedrich

Since the founding of Alternative for Germany (AfD), political scientists, capital city journalists, and the bourgeois feuilleton have sought to comprehend the party's success.[1] The explanations are manifold: at times a supposed shift to the left by the CDU/CSU parties is the cause of the AfD's success, at other times the weakness of the SPD is cited as a contributing factor, still other explanations point to the former existence of the GDR, which is said to have turned the people of East Germany into totalitarian lemmings. The focus then shifts to social groups that are supposedly responsible for this development: "refugees," "Ossis," "workers." These diagnosed causes are largely devoid of a materialist analysis of capitalism.[2] It is worth taking a closer look at partial aspects of some of the popular explanations and placing them in relation to each other so that they can then be analyzed against the backdrop of a crisis in the socialization of capitalism. Six crisis phenomena can be identified which, taken together, constitute the beginnings of a hegemonic crisis. Before turning to these phenomena, it is useful to first consider the character of right-wing movements in recent years.

1 The Right-Wing Project

The analysis of the rise of the right should not be limited to the AfD. Rather, a right-wing hegemonic project that extends beyond the party has been developing for several years.

Hegemonic projects can be summarized as strategies of actors "that in part relate to each other deliberately, but also distinguish themselves from each

---

1 The analysis draws on previous work, in particular Friedrich, 2019.
2 In the left-wing debate, on the other hand, there is now a whole series of materialist analyses dedicated to the recent rise of the right. See for example *Autoritärer Populismus*, 2018; Beck and Stützle, 2018. And worth reading even before the AfD was founded: *Konservatismus/ Ideologie* (2012).

other and would not consider themselves as part of a 'common project (Buckel et al, 2014: 46)."' The various actors involved in this project share similar strategies and objectives to solve the problems they have identified and are united by a common objective to fundamentally transform this society. They maintain contact with actors in Europe, with the right-wing governments in Hungary and Poland providing guidance. Hegemonic projects do not emerge overnight or according to a prefabricated plan; rather, they are formed gradually, for example, through the implementation of concrete political projects that present themselves as a solution to certain social, economic or political crises (Bieling and Steinhilber, 2000: 106). Examples of concrete right-wing political projects include the reinforcement of Germany's borders, the abolition of gender studies chairs, leaving the EU, the reintroduction of the Deutsche Mark or an ignorance of the fight against climate change. "In order for a hegemonic project to become hegemonic, it must succeed in positioning a series of limited political projects in a way that they become the political-strategic "terrain" on which a hegemonic project can consolidate (Buckel et al, 2014: 48)."

In addition to the AfD, other actors involved in the hegemonic project include the media, intellectuals, social movements, the "New Right," fundamentalist Christians, fraternity members, anti-feminist organizations, right-wing libertarians, the nobility, European networks and individual factions of capital.

There are essentially three ideological currents fighting for supremacy within the right-wing project as a whole and the AfD in particular. Firstly, there is the national-conservative line, which includes the weekly newspaper *Junge Freiheit*, anti-feminist networks and Christian fundamentalists who emphasize monogamous marriage between a man and a woman as the central model of life and campaign against equality for gays and lesbians as well as queer lifestyles. Georg Paszderski and Beatrix von Storch are two prominent figures within the AfD who belong to the national-conservative current.

The second ideological current are the national-neoliberals, who played an important role in the founding phase of the AfD. However, even after the departure of initiators such as economics professor Bernd Lucke and former head of the Federation of German Industries Hans-Olaf Henkel, as well as long-time party leader Jörg Meuthen, the AfD's substantive orientation is largely characterized by neo- or ordoliberal positions (Kellershohn, 2019: 91–98). Notable figures within the AfD, including parliamentary group leader and party chairwoman Alice Weidel and deputy chairman Peter Boehringer, can be attributed to the national-neoliberal current. Beyond the AfD, the national neoliberal current is also present in the magazine *eigentümlich frei* and the

Friedrich-August-von-Hayek-Gesellschaft, which itself has moved strongly to the right in recent years (Bidder, 2021).

While national-conservatives and national-neoliberals played a significant role in the founding of the AfD, the influence of the third current only became more pronounced over the course of the party's history. The Völkisch-nationalist current, associated with the figure of Björn Höcke within the party, is ideologically and personally closely linked to the self-proclaimed New Right, a school of thought for the restoration of right-wing thought that developed in the 1960s (Wölk, 2020: 167–230). Alongside these figures, the Völkisch-nationalist current is seeking to close ranks with the streets. At the latest since the Pegida mobilizations in Dresden in fall 2014, it has become evident that this segment of the right has the character of a social movement capable of mobilization.

There are substantial differences between the three currents: for example, there are diverging positions on economic and social policy (Eberhardt and Friedrich, 2019: 113–27). Another point of contention, around which most of the AfD's power and directional struggles have revolved since its foundation, is a strategic issue. While a majority of the actors in the national-conservative and national-neoliberal currents prefer tactical moderation and a parliament-oriented approach, the majority of the Völkisch-nationalist currents rely on a movement-oriented, fundamental oppositional course (Berzel et al, 2017). Despite their differences, all currents adhere to an ideology of inequality. Whether for the collective (as exemplified by the Völkisch current) or the individual (as exemplified by the national neoliberals) – the underlying principle is the same: the superiority of the strong over the weak is a natural phenomenon.

The currents frequently overlap, alliances are frequently formed, individual actors attempt to combine them or cannot be clearly assigned. However, in order to more effectively comprehend the dynamics of the right-wing project, it is beneficial to analytically distinguish the three currents.

The AfD plays a decisive role in the formation of the right, as it provides the platform on which the various ideological factions and actors can gather and discuss their positions. The party functions as a center of gravity for German right-wing extremism (Schulze, 2021: 70).

The AfD's historical significance lies in its capacity as the first serious party in Germany that could succeed in uniting the German right for the first time in decades. It thus takes up where the NSDAP left off, which was the last successful right-wing big tent party in Germany. The AfD is both an expression of the formation of a right-wing hegemonic project as well as its driving force. The party will demonstrate whether the various factions of the right in Germany can collaborate effectively, and which of the currents would be best positioned to assume leadership of the right-wing project.

2   Elements of the Hegemonic Crisis

In contrast to the politicist approach that is prevalent in political science and large parts of political journalism, the search for causes will be approached from a materialist perspective. However, this approach is not to be confused with a derivative materialism, which understands all social formations as a consequence of economic developments. Instead, it is based on a Marxist political analysis that takes the political sphere is taken seriously as a material dimension. Politics possesses "an independent materiality – not only as institutional and discursive materiality, but as a system of constellations of actors and forms of practice in which – in relation to binding decisions for society – the constantly contested 'metabolic process' between state and society is organized (Deppe, 2016: 15)."

The concept of hegemony, as defined by the Italian Marxist Antonio Gramsci, is of paramount importance in this context. The fundamental premise is the idea that in a bourgeois society, the maintenance of existing structures cannot be guaranteed solely through coercion from above but it requires the consent from below. Hegemony describes the capacity of the ruling class to integrate the leading groups of the exploited and oppressed into a historical bloc through compromise. This conception posits that the state is not merely a repressive entity; rather, it is an integral state comprising political society and civil society. It is thus "hegemony, protected by the armour of coercion (Gramsci, 1991: 263)."

The interplay of ideology and repressive apparatuses, which are not decisively economic entities, is the only factor "capable of securing the ownership of the means of production or of abstract wealth, money, its power of command over material and personal resources (Haug, 2012: 135)." A crisis of hegemony is, therefore, above all a crisis of the dominant (and ruling) class, as it no longer reaches the masses, the consensus is no longer shared, and instead is abandoned (Gramsci, 1981: 210).

At the latest since the 2007/2008 financial crisis, there has been a growing discourse surrounding a fundamental crisis of neoliberalism (Institute, 2009) and a crisis of hegemony in Europe (Oberndorfer, 2012: 49–71). This is more than just a cyclical crisis of capitalist valorization; rather, transnational high-tech capitalism is experiencing a fundamental crisis of overaccumulation (Haug, 2012: 25–128). This development is concomitant with a turning point in the imperialist balance of power, in which the US is in danger of losing its role as hegemon (Ibid; Arrighi, 2009).

The first indications of a hegemonic crisis are also becoming apparent in Germany at a time when the existing institutions and prevailing ideologies of society are losing their binding power and new ones have not yet been established. As has often been quoted in recent years, it is the time when "the old is dying and the new cannot be born (Gramsci, 1981: 178)," it is a certain point in history when social groups break away from traditional parties (Ibid: 178, 276), when, unlike in a conjunctural crisis, "incurable contradictions" emerge in a society (Ibid: 178).

The dominant power bloc is divided on a number of issues and parts of the masses refuse to give their consent. The phenomena of such a hegemonic crisis can be observed more clearly in countries such as France (Döll, 2016: 451–57) and the US (Rehmann, 2016). However, indications of such a crisis can also be found in Germany, where the right can benefit from the situation.

The crisis of hegemony has driven the rise of the right, as evidenced by the emergence of six subcrises: the crisis of conservatism, the crisis of representation, the crisis of capital, the decline of social mobility, the crisis of achievement ideology and the crisis of the left.

3   The Split among Conservatives

It is primarily socio-political issues that have gotten conservatives in Germany into trouble in recent years and decades: Immigrants wanted to be more than just tolerated "guests," women more than just wives, and gays, lesbians and queer people more than just deviants. Even the conservative CDU/CSU parties now largely accept that Germany is a country of immigration, and the black-yellow coalition government also decided to phase out nuclear power in 2011. The majority of society is in favor of gender equality and more or less recognizes same-sex love as normal (Küpper et al, 2017).

However, these social developments have been the subject of heated debate in recent years: In August 2010, Thilo Sarrazin published his book *Deutschland schafft sich ab* (Germany abolishes itself), which sold well over a million copies. The book is not only a pamphlet for the rehabilitation of intelligence research, which has been sidelined in Germany, but also an arch-conservative plea for an imagined German guiding culture. With the book's publication, topics such as the integration of immigrants and the role of Islam entered the political and media debate. Despite the lamentations of the left and liberals regarding a socio-political rollback during the controversies, the course and outcome of the events resulted in a defeat from a right-wing perspective. Sarrazin was widely quoted and discussed, yet ultimately, reactionary positions that invoked a German identity based on blood had to accept a loss of significance in the hegemonic discourse. The central criterion for assessing migration has consistently been and continues to be economic exploitability. The racism associated with Völkisch nationalism has receded in significance relative to the racism of neoliberal meritocracy (Friedrich, 2011: 8–38).

A crisis of the old conservatism can also be seen in women's and family policy. Here, too, it was a book that initially boosted such positions. Back in September 2006, Eva Herman, a television presenter at the time, published *Das Eva-Prinzip* (The Eva Principle), in which she argued for a reactionary distribution of roles: men were not meant to raise children due to their biological disposition, in contrast to women, who should focus on their "natural" abilities (Herman, 2006: 59).

Although Herman and Sarrazin mobilized the (national) conservative segment of the population and were able to garner one or two approving statements from sections of the CDU/CSU parties, the reality beyond symbolic politics in the form of laws and reforms speaks a different language. The discussion surrounding Herman's book coincided with a clear turnaround in the CDU's family policy orientation. During her tenure as Federal Minister for Family Affairs between 2005 and 2009, Ursula von der Leyen encountered significant opposition from within her own party over several initiatives, including her advocacy for a relatively modernized family model. For instance, following a contentious debate, she succeeded in securing the legal right to nursery places.

The discourse surrounding Eva Herman and the comparatively progressive family policy of the CDU/CSU has precipitated a divide among conservatives. As a consequence of the debate, various anti-feminist initiatives have been established, including the far-right organization free gender and the Initiative Agens as part of a men's rights movement.

The CDU/CSU policy – analogous to the modernized immigration policy – is economically justified: The dissolution of the traditional breadwinner family, the politically promoted "emancipation" and the compulsion for gainful employment to which every individual is exposed must be viewed in the context of neoliberal deregulation and the expansion of the low-wage sector, which in turn comes at the expense of women and immigrant workers (Lent and Trumann, 2015).

While the CDU/CSU largely abandoned its role as the guardian of German customs and the traditional division of gender roles and revamped itself in socio-political terms, discourses on immigration, integration, the role of women and sexual diversity increasingly emerged on the far right, seeking to fill the gap created by the modernization of the CDU/CSU.

4 Discomfort with Parliamentary Democracy

The gradual erosion of parliamentary democracy and the alignment of established parties also favors the formation of the right-wing project. The crisis of parliamentarianism is expressed in the declining voter turnout over decades: While more than 90 percent of those eligible to vote participated in the 1970s German Federal Republic (FRG) elections, voter turnout in the 2017 Bundestag election was 76 percent, and in 2013 and 2009 it was only around 71 percent. Loyalty to established parties has also declined sharply: since 1990, the membership of both the SPD and the CDU has almost halved. Moreover, 60% of respondents do not view the local form of government as a true democracy, given that economic influence is perceived to be too dominant (Schroeder and Deutz-Schroeder, 2015: 568–69).

The rejection of party organizations and parliamentary representation, in addition to doubts about democracy, are indicative of Colin Crouch's diagnosis of a "post-democracy," according to which there is a growing trend of eroding democratic institutions by business elites, resulting in an ever increasing concentration of power in their hands (Crouch, 2004). Criticism of the established parties, the prevailing political system and, to some extent, the media can be interpreted as a reaction to developments of an increasingly isolating political class. This class makes far-reaching decisions "overnight" in bodies that lack democratic legitimacy, for which long parliamentary debates and social disputes used to be necessary in the years past. Instead, the political class is all too happy to justify its decisions by pointing to a supposed lack of alternatives.

This phenomenon is not exclusive to neoliberal capitalism, but is a basic principle of parliamentary democracy in capitalist societies. In parliamentarism, social contradictions and the class question are reduced to a mere pluralism of interests. Consequently, parties no longer represent the interests of certain groups, they "separate themselves from their own social basis and become part of political state associations," writes Johannes Agnoli (1967: 33).[3] Ultimately, it is about the struggle for power between different ruling elites. Democracy is affected by a process of regression and erosion, which can be described as an "involution." This results in a situation where the term "democracy without

---

3 For an English-language summary and supplement, see Agnoli, 2014.

demos" is used to describe the current state of affairs (Ibid: 44)." In this context, parliament becomes a "transmission belt for the decisions of oligarchal groups (Ibid: 68)." Consequently, the state gradually transforms into an authoritarian state. Accordingly, it is not parliamentarism itself that is destroyed, because democracy continues to exist formally, but the clash of interests is blocked.

It is not only left-wingers who criticize post-democratic conditions. Since the 1980s, so-called right-wing populism has emphasized that the current democracy no longer works. Right-wingers distance themselves from "those up there," which primarily refers to politicians in Brussels. Concurrently, right-wing populist criticism of democracy also positions itself against "those down there:" Immigrants, people from Eastern and Southern Europe or the unemployed (Reinfeldt, 2013: 35). "Those at the top are more likely to govern in an unjust manner, as they lack sufficient legitimacy to represent the 'overwhelming majority' of the population. This is a rhetorical figure of repulsion (Ibid: 53)."

A situation characterized by post-democratic discomfort is therefore conducive to the establishment of a dualism between "the people" and "the politicians." This dualism, which fails to address the economic preconditions that facilitate social power shifts, is a defining feature of right-wing populist politics. The juxtaposition of "the people" and "politics" is expressed not only in the demand for referendums and in the rejection of the "old parties," but even in the party's name. For instance, "Alternative for Germany" draws its name from the inflationary use of the political buzzword "no alternative (alternativlos)" which Angela Merkel has increasingly utilized since 2009.

5 Disunity among Factions of Capital

The crisis of conservatism and political representation coincides with a crisis of neoliberal capitalism While there has been a decline in approval of the current form of capitalism, parallel to growing inequality in society, the internal contradictions between different factions of capital are becoming more visible.

The neoliberal variety of capitalism became the predominant form of the economy and socialization after the first global economic crisis since World War II at the end of the 1970s. "Neoliberalism is in the first instance a theory of political economic practices positing that human well-being can best be advanced by unleashing the entrepreneurial freedoms and skills of individuals within an institutional framework characterized by robust private property rights, free markets, and free trade (Harvey, 2005: 2)." As an ideology, neoliberalism goes far beyond economic and social policy issues. In recent decades, it has become the central morality that fundamentally shapes the way we think. As one scholar put it, "Neoliberalism seeks the entire personality, the entire person, lock, stock and barrel (Schreiner, 2018: 108)."

At the latest since the 2007 economic crisis, neoliberalism has been forced to confront with its own internal contradictions (Bader et al, 2011: 11–28). Even if the prevailing financial and economic policy quickly realigned itself along supply-oriented principles, as evidenced by the EU's fiscal and austerity policies, contradictions between the neoliberal policies of the EU and the national neoliberals in Germany, who were more oriented towards national sovereignty, became apparent in the course of the fight against the Euro crisis. "The disputes over crisis management have enormously deepened the contradictions within the ruling classes, particularly in the EU. In the countries with balance of payments surpluses, dissent is primarily driven by the mutualization of liability for the national debt of eurozone member states (Prokla-Redaktion, 2016: 524)."

The underlying conflict is rooted in competing interests: The EU, and the European Central Bank (ECB) in its central position, are primarily concerned with the economy of the entire eurozone. In the event of uncertainty, they must override the specific interests of German capital, despite the significant influence of the German government. National neoliberals are therefore skeptical of non-governmental institutions and rely on stability politics within the national framework.

In principle, companies compete with one other under capitalism, but for decades, large sections of capital formed a kind of political unity and articulated their interests collectively. In the meantime, the factions of capital have become increasingly differentiated and diverging interests have become apparent. In particular, the contradictions between corporations that operate on European and global markets and companies that are far more oriented towards regional and local sales markets are relevant for the analysis of the AfD.

Globally oriented capital can react more flexibly to more favorable location conditions in other countries, regions and continents. These different conditions result in conflicting interests. For example, an export-oriented company benefits from the European Single Market as well as from the Euro, which is relatively inexpensive compared to the D-Mark, because it strengthens its competitiveness. On the other hand, for a company that produces for the domestic market, it makes no significant difference whether the goods are paid for in Euros or D-Marks.

In particular, between 2009 and 2013, fissures began to appear in the European policy of the German power bloc. In contrast to export capital, the Family Business Association was fundamentally opposed to Germany's Euro rescue policy during the Euro crisis, advocated "a further tightening of fiscal policy measures," opposed "any form of Europeanization of economic policy" and resorted to "some right-wing populist rhetoric (Heine and Sablowski, 2013: 31)."

The German government engaged in debate regarding key positions held by national neoliberals until summer 2012. However, following protracted internal disputes, the black-yellow coalition government ultimately opted to prioritize the deepening of European economic integration. By the time the European Stability Mechanism (ESM) was adopted and the ECB bought back government bonds, it was clear that the exclusion of Greece was off the table and the demand for a flexible monetary union could not be implemented with the existing government. National neoliberals had suffered a severe defeat and reoriented themselves, moving beyond their traditional parties, namely CDU, CSU and FDP. Economists around Bernd Lucke substantiated their plans to form a new party.

6 Growing Inequality in a Society of Downward Mobility

The population's dwindling approval of the current system is another expression of an emerging hegemonic crisis. In 1992, the associations with capitalism were far more positive than in 2012. While 48% of respondents associated it with "freedom" in the early 1990s, this figure had fallen to 27% in 2012, while 69% thought of "progress" in 1992 and only 38% in 2012. In contrast, the association with "exploitation" rose from 66% to 77% (Köcher, 2012: 5).

The subjective dissatisfaction with capitalism has its basis in reality – the gap between rich and poor in Germany continued to widen until midway through the last decade (Goebel et al, 2015: 571). The "golden age" of capitalism (Hobsbawm, 1995: 225–402) in the "Western" countries is over and rates of profit are falling worldwide (Nachtwey, 2018: 33–57).

With the unsuccessful neoliberal attempts to open up new markets through deregulation and privatization and thus stabilize renewed growth, the pressure on wage labor increased, wages fell continuously, "flexibilization" increased competition between workers, and the low-wage sector and precarious employment relations have consolidated (Ibid: 86–93). At the same time, the socio-political liberalizations described above were implemented. These processes of regressive modernization

> frequently combine social liberalization with economic deregulation. Horizontally, between groups with different sexual orientations, between

genders and in certain respects even between ethnic communities, society has become more egalitarian and inclusive – but vertically, this egalitarianism is tied to greater economic inequalities.

Ibid: 5

Concurrently, precarious employment relations are on the rise, and not just among sections of the working class. There is an "'elevated' form of precarity" among those who are skilled to highly skilled (Castel, 2009: 32). The employment relationships of mid-level academics, self-employed individuals engaged in creative professions, and educators, for instance, are characterized by fixed-term contracts, uncertain future prospects, and exceptionally high flexibility requirements.

The so-called middle of society, the middle classes are also coming under pressure: Upward mobility is increasingly being replaced by the risk of social decline and concerns about the economic situation within the middle class have increased significantly in Germany, particularly during the first decade of the 21st century (Bertelsmann Stiftung, 2012) – a development that has been evident in the lower-income middle class in rich countries for the past three decades (Milanović, 2016: 17–20).

Among segments of the middle class and upper echelon of the working class, this phenomenon has given rise to a nebulous rejection of the status quo while concurrently underscoring the assertion of privileges. A confluence of the post-democratic unease delineated above and fears of decline characterizes the disaffected "mainstream." Even in the years preceding the advent of the AfD, social scientists repeatedly posited that authoritarianism and racism are pervasive and that there is a general shift to the right in mainstream society. In 2010, there was a significant increase in derogatory, misanthropic attitudes towards various vulnerable groups, particularly among higher income groups (Groß et al, 2010: 146–47). On this basis, a 2014 study showed that parts of the middle classes are in favor of "market-based extremism (Groß and Hövermann, 2014: 106)." In addition to the generalized norm of self-optimization, this includes the demand for omnipresent competition and an economistic mindset in which population groups are evaluated according to cost-benefit criteria (Ibid: 109). Support for market-based extremism is twice as high among people who perceive a threat to their standard of living and savings than among those who do not (Ibid: 111). "The AfD party is evidently capitalizing on the existing potential for populist rhetoric as a political platform, particularly in its economic misanthropic undertones. Among those who espouse the AfD's arguments, market-based extremism and feelings of threat and insecurity are particularly prevalent (Ibid: 118)."

7 The Disintegration of Achievement Ideology

The growing inequality in a society of downward mobility has intensified a classist discourse on the middle of society. Many of those who consider themselves to be in the middle of society try to differentiate themselves from those at the bottom, from those who "refuse to perform (Baron and Steinwachs, 2012)."

The growing tendency to cite achieved and potentially unappreciated performance also suggests that an increasing number of individuals are becoming aware that performance is not a worthwhile pursuit (Dröge et al, 2005: 368–74). The attainment of one's personal objectives is not contingent upon one's own efforts, but rather upon factors such as chance, social background, and other elements that are largely beyond one's control. The ideological tenets upon which the achievement society was built are no longer holding firm.

The realization that performance does not necessarily lead to success can prompt reactionary approaches to crisis resolution. If chance and origin ultimately determine one's life prospects, these factors must be leveraged in the best possible way. For instance, if gender, citizenship, and social background are relevant factors of influence in this society, they can be utilized: If one is no longer able to win, but is threatened with decline in all areas, then at least one should strive to defend one's position.

Consequently, right-wing workers tend to "fight the battle to maintain and improve their status with the help of resentment (Dörre et al, 2018: 58)." Universal solidarity is replaced by a competitive mindset. Workers are upgrading themselves by devaluing old and new ethnic milieus within the working class. The right's thematization of the social question is an attempt to "give an ethnic-nationalist format to the test of wages and working conditions (Ibid: 56)." In short: the elbow replaces the fist.[4]

Cultural conservatism, nationalism, racism and sexism thus meet heightened competition and real fears of decline, which are primarily processed within neoliberal ways of thinking – achievement ideology and economistic (self-)evaluation. This is how the explosive mixture comes about: the right-wing culture war and real material concerns form an excellent basis for processing fears of decline in a reactionary way.

The focus of these struggles is not on securing higher wages, opposing precarious employment relations, or advocating for redistribution. Instead, these struggles are directed against other groups on the domestic and global labor

---

4 See the contribution by Bafta Sarbo in this volume, pp. 37–63.

market. The phenomenon of desolidarization and exclusive solidarity represents a response to intensified competitive conditions under capitalism. These responses do not challenge or destabilize the fundamental systemic principles or neoliberal ideology, which serves to maintain the dominance of the ruling class.

At least part of the "middle" in crisis thus resembles a cyclist, as Kurt Tucholsky described him almost a century ago: They subserviently and respectfully raise their heads upwards, while pontifically pedaling downwards. This is an incisive pattern of how real questions are answered in a reactionary way (Tucholsky, 1958: 155).

8 The Crisis of the Left

While the power bloc is crumbling at the levels outlined above, the left in society as a whole has been in a deep crisis for decades. Above all, the collapse of the Soviet Union had a profound impact on the socialist left, regardless of the hopes or criticisms associated with actually existing socialism. The social democrat Peter von Oertzen, who was not a friend of the Soviet Union, provided an apt summary of the dire situation even for social democracy in the autumn of 1990, even before the dissolution of the Soviet Union:

> The left in the 'West' is trying to wrest ecological reason, social justice and economic democracy from a capitalism that is only held in check by a limited democracy and the welfare state; but it is met with scorn – even from within its own ranks: 'What do you fools want? Gorbachev is abolishing socialism in the East and you want to reintroduce it in the West.
> VON OERTZEN, 1990; HOFSCHEN, 1991: 217?

Social democracy was able to maintain its position for a few years after 1989, at least in name, due to its increasing neoliberalization in the wake of New Labour and the new social democracy, it had taken a momentous turn. Today, social democratic parties are in decline in many European states, in part because social democracy is now part of the "extreme center (Ali, 2015)." In Europe, North America and Australia, this "extreme center" ranges from traditional center-left to center-right parties. The "extreme center" wages war externally and also goes to war internally by means of austerity against its own population. The conservative, liberal and social democratic parties can hardly be distinguished in terms of their specific policies, as is evidenced by the ongoing crisis of parliamentary democracy.

The "extreme center" in Germany has completed the cultural modernization of society. It is reasonably progressive in socio-political terms, but in economic and social policy terms it relies on competition and individual willingness to perform. It has given priority to the interests of export-oriented capital, improved the "location conditions" at the expense of wage earners and at the same time launched dazzling diversity programs. The ideal state embodiment of "progressive neoliberalism (Fraser, 2017)" was the red-green coalition government from 1998 to 2005. As a kind of left wing of the "extreme center," it combined a culturally semi-progressive program with a strictly right-wing economic and social policy agenda: the red-green government combined the reform of citizenship law and the introduction of civil partnership with a radical restructuring of the welfare state in line with the interests of capital, including a significant reduction of the maximum tax rate. In nominal terms the most left-wing government ever to be formed in the Federal Republic of Germany, it was also the government that initiated the normalization of military operations. Subsequent governments have essentially continued this red-green course.

The crisis of the left goes to the very core, to the very foundations of what are considered the cornerstones of leftism are, as can be seen, for example, in an increasingly misleading discussion about identity politics, in which class politics on the one hand and anti-racism or feminism on the other are placed in competition with each other. Left-wing – or more precisely: socialist – politics means taking up both: the struggle for freedom on a socio-political level and the struggle for equality on a social and economic level – or as US feminist Nancy Fraser demands in relation to the US: to reject the false alternative of progressive neoliberalism and reactionary populism. "We should link the harms suffered by women and people of color to those experienced by the many who voted for Trump. In that way, a revitalized left could lay the foundation for a powerful new coalition committed to fighting for all (Ibid)."

From the standpoint of analyzing the rise of the right against the backdrop of a nascent hegemonic crisis, it follows from a socialist perspective that the crisis of capitalism should be the starting point. It is possible that the left will succeed in re-establishing its identity through the newfound strength of the right. Indeed, this is an urgent necessity, given that there are numerous indications that the hegemonic crisis, to which the right owes its rise, is deepening. It is imperative that a socialist project identifies and implements solutions to the root causes of this crisis.

Bibliography

Agnoli, Johannes (1967) *Die Transformation der Demokratie*. Berlin: Voltaire Verlag.

Agnoli, Johannes (2014) Theses on the Transformation of Democracy and on the Extra-Parliamentary Opposition, *Viewpoint Magazine*, Oct. 12, viewpointmag.com/2014/10/12/theses-on-the-transformation-of-democracy-and-on-the-extra-parliamentary-opposition.

Ali, Tariq (2015) *The Extreme Centre: A Warning*. London: Verso.

Arrighi, Giovanni (2009) *Die verschlungenen Pfade des Kapitals. Ein Gespräch mit David Harvey, Analysen mit Beverly J. Silver zur Weltgeschichte der Arbeiterbewegung und zu China*. Hamburg: Argument Verlag.

Autoritärer Populismus. Strategie und politische Ökonomie rechter Politik (2018) Prokla vol. 48, no. 190.

Bader, Pauline et al. (2011) Die multiple Krise. Krisendynamiken im neoliberalen Kapitalismus. In: Pauline Bader et al. (eds.), *VielfachKrise. Im finanzmarktdominierten Kapitalismus*. Hamburg: VSA Verlag.

Baron, Christian and Britta Steinwachs (2012) *"Faul, Frech, Dreist." Die Diskriminierung von Erwerbslosigkeit durch BILD-Leser*innen*. Münster: edition assemblage.

Beck, Martin and Ingo Stützle (2018) *Die neuen Bonapartisten. Mit Marx den Aufstieg von Trump und Co. verstehen*. Berlin: Karl Dietz Verlag.

Bertelsmann Stiftung (2012) Mittelschicht schrumpft seit 15 Jahren. *Bertelsmann Stiftung*, bertelsmann-stiftung.de/de/unsere-projekte/abgeschlossene-projekte/wirtschaftliche-dynamik-und-beschaeftigung/projektnachrichten/mittelschicht-schrumpft-seit-15-jahren.

Berzel, Alexander et al. (2017) Parlamentarische Praxis der AfD in deutschen Landesparlamenten, *WZB Discussion Paper SP V 2017–102*, Berlin.

Bidder, Benjamin (2021) Mangelnde Abgrenzung nach rechts. AfD-Streit zerreißt liberale Hayek-Gesellschaft, *Der Spiegel*, Jan. 31, spiegel.de/wirtschaft/afd-streit-zerreisst-liberale-hayek-gesellschaft-a-cee3c3af-41ff-4214-8223-bfce080825fe.

Bieling, Hans-Jürgen and Jochen Steinhilber (2000) Hegemoniale Projekte im Prozess der europäischen Integration. In: Bieling and Steinhilber (eds.), *Die Konfiguration Europas. Dimensionen einer kritischen Integrationstheorie*. Münster: Westfälisches Dampfboot.

Buckel, Sonja et al. (2014) Historisch-materialistische Politikanalyse. Die Operationalisierung materialistischer Staatstheorie für die empirische Forschung. In: Forschungsgruppe "Staatsprojekt Europa" (eds.), *Kämpfe um Migrationspolitik. Theorie, Methode und Analysen kritischer Europaforschung* Bielefeld: transcript Verlag.

Castel, Robert (2009) Die Wiederkehr der sozialen Unsicherheit. In: Robert Castel and Klaus Dörre (eds.), *Prekarität, Abstieg, Ausgrenzung. Die soziale Frage am Beginn des 21. Jahrhunderts*. Frankfurt am Main: campus Verlag.

Crouch, Colin (2004) *Post-Democracy*. Cambridge: Polity Press.
Deppe, Frank (2016) *Politisches Denken im 20. Jahrhundert, Band 1: Die Anfänge*. Hamburg: VSA Verlag.
Döll, David (2016) Die Strategie der convergence des luttes in Frankreich. Zur Bewegungsdynamik zwischen Demokratie- und Klassenfrage, *Prokla* vol. 46, no. 184.
Dörre, Klaus et al. (2018) Arbeiterbewegung von rechts? Motive und Grenzen einer imaginären Revolte, *Berliner Journal für Soziologie*, vol. 28.
Dröge, Kai et al. (2005) Das umkämpfte Leistungsprinzip. Deutungskonflikte um die Legitimationen sozialer Ungleichheit, *WSI Mitteilungen*, vol. 7.
Eberhardt, Simon and Sebastian Friedrich (2019) Der Kampf zweier Linien. Wirtschafts- und sozialpolitische Konzepte im rechten Projekt. In: Andrea Becker et al. (eds.), *Zwischen Neoliberalismus und völkischem "Antikapitalismus." Sozial- und wirtschaftspolitische Konzepte und Debatten innerhalb der AfD*. Münster: Unrast Verlag.
Fraser, Nancy (2017) Für eine neue Linke oder: Das Ende des progressiven Neoliberalismus, *Blätter für deutsche und internationale Politik*, vol. 2, pp. 71–76, blaetter.de/ausgabe/2017/februar/fuer-eine-neue-linke-oder-das-ende-des-progres siven-neoliberalismus.
Friedrich, Sebastian (2019) *Die AfD. Analysen, Hintergründe, Kontroversen*. Berlin: Bertz und Fischer.
Friedrich, Sebastian (2011) Rassismus in der Leistungsgesellschaft. Einleitung. In: Sebastian Friedrich (ed.), *Rassismus in der Leistungsgesellschaft. Analysen und kritische Perspektiven zu den rassistischen Normalisierungsprozessen der "Sarrazindebatte."* Münster: edition assemblage, 2011.
Goebel, Jan et al. (2015) Einkommensungleichheit in Deutschland bleibt weiterhin hoch – junge Alleinlebende und Berufseinsteiger sind zunehmend von Armut bedroht, *DIW Wochenbericht*, vol. 25.
Gramsci, Antonio (1981) *Selections from the Prison Notebooks*. New York: International Publishers.
Groß, Eva and Andreas Hövermann (2014) Marktförmiger Extremismus – ein Phänomen der Mitte? In: Andreas Zick and Anna Klein (eds.), *Fragile Mitte – Feindselige Zustände. Rechtsextreme Einstellungen in Deutschland*. Bonn: Verlag J.H.W. Dietz.
Groß, Eva et al. (2010) Die Ökonomisierung der Gesellschaft. Ein Nährboden für Menschenfeindlichkeit in oberen Status- und Einkommensgruppen. In: Wilhelm Heitmeyer (ed.), *Deutsche Zustände. Folge 9*. Berlin: Suhrkamp Verlag.
Harvey, David (2005) *A Brief History of Neoliberalism*. New York: Oxford University Press.
Haug, Wolfgang Fritz (2012) *Hightech-Kapitalismus in der großen Krise*. Hamburg: Argument Verlag.
Heine, Frederic and Thomas Sablowski (2013) *Die Europapolitik des deutschen Machtblocks und ihre Widersprüche. Eine Untersuchung der Positionen deutscher Wirtschaftsverbände zur Eurokrise*. Berlin: Rosa-Luxemburg-Stiftung.

Herman, Eva (2006) *Das Eva-Prinzip. Für eine neue Weiblichkeit.* München and Zürich: Pendo Verlag.

Hobsbawm, Eric (1995) *The Age of Extremes: The Short Twentieth Century 1914–1991.* London: Abacus.

Hofschen, Heinz-Gerd (1991) "Ein sehr notwendiges Stück Arbeit." Die gegenwärtige Niederlage des Sozialismus und die Geschichtsschreibung der Arbeiterbewegung. In: Manfred Bobke-von Camen et al., *Der Trümmerhaufen als Aussichtsturm. Historische, aktuelle und perspektivische Vermessungen einer gründlich veränderten Situation.* Marburg: Verlag Arbeit & Gesellschaft.

Institute of Society Analysis of Rosa-Luxemburg-Foundation (2009) The crisis of finance market capitalism – challenge for the left, *kontrovers – Beiträge zur politischen Bildung* vol. 1, rosalux.de/fileadmin/rls_uploads/pdfs/engl/kontovers_01-2009_short-en.pdf.

Kellershohn, Helmut (2019) Nationaler Wettbewerbsstaat auf völkischer Basis in einem ‚Europa der Nationen.' Die Programmatik der AfD seit 2016. In: Andrea Becker et al. (eds.), *Zwischen Neoliberalismus und völkischem "Antikapitalismus." Sozial- und wirtschaftspolitische Konzepte und Debatten innerhalb der AfD.* Münster: Unrast Verlag.

Köcher, Renate (2012) Das Unbehagen am Kapitalismus, *Frankfurter Allgemeine Zeitung*, Feb. 22.

Konservatismus/Ideologie (2012) *Z – Zeitschrift marxistische Erneuerung,* vol. 90.

Küpper, Beate et al. (2017) *Einstellungen gegenüber Lesben, Schwulen und Bisexuellen in Deutschland. Ergebnisse einer bevölkerungsrepräsentativen Umfrage.* Baden-Baden: Nomos.

Lent, Lilli and Andrea Trumann, (2015) *Kritik des Staatsfeminismus.* Berlin: Bertz und Fischer.

Milanović, Branko (2016) *Die ungleiche Welt. Migration, Das Eine Prozent und die Zukunft der Mittelschicht.* Berlin: Suhrkamp Verlag.

Nachtwey, Oliver (2018) *Germany's Hidden Crisis: Social Decline in the Heart of Europe.* London: Verso.

Oberndorfer, Lukas (2012) Hegemoniekrise in Europa – Auf dem Weg zu einem autoritären Wettbewerbsetatismus. In: Forschungsgruppe "Staatsprojekt Europa" (eds.), *Die EU in der Krise.* Münster: Westfälisches Dampfboot.

Prokla-Redaktion (2016) Der globale Kapitalismus im Ausnahmezustand, *Prokla* vol. 46, no. 185.

Rehmann, Jan (2016) Bernie Sanders und die Hegemoniekrise des neoliberalen Kapitalismus, *LuXemburg Online*, zeitschrift-luxemburg.de/bernie-sanders-und-die-hegemoniekrise-des-neoliberalen-kapitalismus.

Reinfeldt, Sebastian (2013) *"Wir für Euch." Die Wirksamkeit des Rechtspopulismus in Zeiten der Krise.* Münster: Unrast Verlag.

Sarrazin, Thilo (2010) *Deutschland schafft sich ab. Wir wir unser Land aufs Spiel setzen.* München: Deutsche Verlags-Anstalt.

Schreiner, Patrick (2018) *Unterwerfung als Freiheit. Leben im Neoliberalismus.* Köln: PapyRossa Verlag.

Schroeder, Klaus and Monika Deutz-Schroeder (2015) *Gegen Staat und Kapital – für die Revolution! Linksextremismus in Deutschland – eine empirische Studie.* Frankfurt am Main: Peter Lang Verlag.

Schulze, Christoph (2021) *Rechtsextremismus. Gestalt und Geschichte.* Wiesbaden: Marix Verlag, 2021.

Tucholsky, Kurt (1958) *... ganz anders.* Berlin: Verlag Volk und Welt.

von Oertzen, Peter (1990) Was bleibt von der sozialistischen Vision? *Lecture manuscript*, September.

Wölk, Volkmar (2020) Alter Faschismus in neuen Schläuchen. Auf den Spuren der ‚Neuen' Rechten: Ideologische Zeitreise von Dresden nach Italien und zurück. In: Friedrich Burschel (ed.), *Das faschistische Jahrhundert. Neurechte Diskurse zu Abendland, Identität, Europa und Neoliberalismus.* Berlin: Verbrecher Verlag.

CHAPTER 9

Class and Racism: Notes for an Updated Understanding of Marxism

Eleonora Roldán Mendívil

> The world splits into serfs and rulers.
> Many come last, some come first.
> There are no good reasons for the bad.
> That is why I continue to write anthems for the serfs.
> DISARSTAR, GLÜCKSSCHMIED

∴

Racism is a complex subject area. In nine contributions, seven authors have addressed specific questions on the historical genesis and dialectical-materialist reality of racist formations in Germany's current class relations. The main conclusions will be summarized in the following article, followed by an outlook for theory and practice.

A fundamental premise of Marxist critique of racism is that the concrete forms that racism takes in a particular historical and geographical context must always be set in relation to capital, because the world is comprehensively determined by the relations of capital. The point is not to derive racist formations deterministically from the capital relation, but to explain the specific form of racism with the tools of dialectical materialism. This account aims to explain the roots of this relationship in concrete terms by analyzing its historical genesis and thus to transcend the merely empirical description of racism.

The analytical derivations in the first part of the volume identify racism, gender and migration and border regimes in their multidimensionality as fundamental to an understanding of modern class societies. Bafta Sarbo's explanation of the concept of racism from a Marxist perspective draws on and updates formal analysis and anti-colonial theorizing. The conditions for the existence of racism must therefore be explained in terms of the relations of production in society. It is the economic relationship that manifests itself in racial difference and produces inequality. The structures of legitimization behind the forms of super-exploitation affecting specifically racialized people thus do not serve an abstract power interest, but follow a specific economic logic of domination.

The independent existence that genocidal racism assumes in certain crisis situations, for example, no longer fulfils a direct material exploitation purpose for capital, since it eliminates labor. A Marxist concept of racism thus demystifies the nature of *race* and racism (Reed Jr, 2013: 49), historicizes these social formations and demonstrates the potential for overcoming them.

On this basis, together with Hannah Vögele, we explain the extent to which the sphere of production and reproduction of human labor takes on a gendered and racialized form. We highlight why an understanding of this specific social division of labor and allocation of people is an elementary component of a precise Marxist social analysis. Programs for the integration of immigrant women into the German labor market usually focus on areas of low-paid reproductive labor, such as the care sector. With reference to Sara R. Farris' concept of femonationalism, these integration and labor market regimes can be understood as being determined by Germany's feminist-nationalist location interests. These programs for the integration of migrant women into the German labor market usually focus on specific areas that are predominantly located in the context of low-paid reproductive work, for example in the care sector. This exposes the invisible hand of the market at the macro level of the state. Programs marketed under the banner of feminism can therefore be conceptualized as transgenerational German location policy, as the focus is on child-rearing and the care of the elderly.

Understanding relations of domination as relations of re/production also plays a central role in Fabian Georgi's analysis of European migration and border regimes. The respective surges in various forms of racism during the crisis of imperialism since 2015 demonstrate how extra-European and extra-territorialized border regimes react to discussions of anti-racist struggles within Germany. Georgi also illustrates how racism fulfills a psychological function: Social participation in the surplus product of an imperialist mode of production negotiated in Germany should only benefit certain people – namely: working Germans. This justifies the super-exploitation of parts of the working class in Germany. This ideology in turn fuels nationalist and/or racist legislation and discourse, which in turn impacts people's daily material lives. It leads to class division into groups with different starting conditions in the free market economy.

Marxist debates on identity and intersectionality are considerably more advanced in the Anglo-Saxon world than in Germany. The prominent position of the US as an imperialist center means that radical perspectives on the specific forms that (super)exploitation assumes today are often first discussed among the US left. Together with Bafta Sarbo, we examine the use of the class concept in two key texts of the intersectionality debate. On this basis, we discuss the key premises of intersectionality theory with particular reference to Marxist critiques from the English-speaking world. We also address the reification of social categories and thereby set the stage to debunk buzzwords such as diversity or plurality. These are repeated almost mantra-like by a broad spectrum of individuals and groups, ranging from the bourgeois to radical left. As Adolph Reed aptly describes, these buzzwords are used to legitimate the "[r]igorous pursuit of equality of opportunity exclusively within the terms of given patterns of capitalist class relations (Ibid: 53)." We can therefore only agree with the critique of intersectionalism by Christin Bernhold, Felix Eckert and John Lütten, who write: "The critique must be directed at the political-theoretical agenda of intersectionalism, rather than at the goal of bringing together struggles against class relations and oppression to include as many people as possible (Benhold et al, 2021: 29)." In the second part of the book, Lea Pilone, Celia Bouali and Sebastian Friedrich turn their attention to the German police, intra-European labor migration and the rise of the right in Germany. Lea Pilone examines the significance of specific control mechanisms towards racialized population groups – such as Roma, Sinti and Jews – for the emergence of the police system in Germany during the transition from feudalism to capitalist class society. It becomes apparent that the police emerged as the guardians of capital interests with the help of racist population policies. As such, racism is not a problem of individual German police officers, but a constantly changing structural prerequisite of police work under capitalist class relations.

The topic of intra-European labor migration is often overlooked in public discussions about racism. In her contribution, Celia Bouali demonstrates how a complex network of national and EU legislation enables Eastern and Southern European immigrants to become pawns of various European capital interests and a flexible, precarious reserve army. It is evident that the deplorable working and living conditions of (seasonal) EU immigrants in Germany are a consequence of location policy interests, rather than the particular ruthlessness of certain shareholders. The causes of this specific form of super-exploitation therefore lie primarily in a legal system that creates a parallel society for EU immigrants in order to extract the maximum surplus value from their labor in the shortest possible time.

Based on these forms of capital accumulation and class compositions, which are constantly changing, Sebastian Friedrich analyzes how openly racist right-wing projects have been able to establish themselves more broadly in Germany in recent years. Through various surges in racism, a *Völkisch*-nationalist racism has increasingly developed into a racism of the neoliberal achievement society. Although the former is still present, the latter is now a determining factor in the right-wing hegemonic project: a racism that focuses on integration/assimilation and performance for the benefit of the German collective. Against the backdrop of falling profit rates, increasing inequality in the German society of downward mobility and a politically weak left, a rich fertile ground for right-wing politics has emerged.

1   On Updating Marxism

The dialectical method is a scientific tool. It is omnipotent and true insofar as it understands society and history in constant movement and in relation to its own conditions and contradictions (Lenin, 1977: 23). It constantly relates all social relations and forms to the nature of the material production of life. Marxism is therefore a suitable instrument to understand social change. Moreover, it is essentially undogmatic, because its critique always arises from the initial conditions of the respective period. Consequently, it does not exclude the left itself, which is also a product of these conditions. As a consequence, Marxism must therefore also constantly innovate in its confrontation with the changing relations of production and class societies. This continued development does not mean throwing Marx or Engels overboard; rather, it means adapting and expanding Marxist critique to make it fruitful for the specific issues of today. Adherence to the dogma of party politics from the 1920s, 1930s or, for example, the 1970s – a time in which the question of Black and indigenous workers' liberation and organization was increasingly being discussed in the Americas, Europe and Africa – would be tantamount to paralysis, which contradicts the dialectical method. For instance, C.L.R. James (Breitman, 1967), Walter Rodney (1975) and José Carlos Mariátegui (1974: 43–49) have provided invaluable insights into the interconnection between capitalism and racism, particularly in relation to the Black Question and the Indigenous Question. Despite all their profound observations for their time, however, their analyses cannot simply be translated into a political program for combating racism in the present day.

The social order is undergoing transformation. New power relations are emerging, and the achievements of the left are being lost once again due to the historical failure of an international proletarian revolution. The analyses and policies that we, as Marxists, are advancing today are situated in the shadow of the collapse of actually existing socialism. Furthermore, they are part of a tradition of political parties and organizations that, in the name of Marxism-Leninism, Trotskyism, Maoism, Guevarism, Pan-Africanism, and Western Marxism, have advanced policies that have bequeathed us a wild mixture of progressive and regressive elements. The study of Marxist methodology necessitates a critical engagement with this tradition.

Nevertheless, the social foundations that led Marx and Engels to formulate the primacy of production in the nineteenth century remain unchanged. Our time is characterized by several interconnected developments, as Barbara Foley aptly summarizes:

> One is the world-historical (if in the long run temporary) defeat of movements to set up and consolidate worker-run egalitarian societies, primarily in China and the USSR. Another – hardly independent of the first – is the neoliberal assault upon the standard of living of the world's workers, as well as upon those unions that have historically supplied a ground for a class-based and class-conscious resistance to capital.
>
> FOLEY, 2018

The new social movements and the efficacy of identity-based political projects represent an important political expression of the changed economic situation and the shortcomings of socialist politics. In Germany, too, class-based resistance to capital has been displaced by non-class-based reformist struggles and movements in recent decades. The "retreat from class (Ibid)" as a central category of social criticism – in liberal as well as radical circles – is therefore not surprising. Nevertheless, we continue to live under the yoke of profit maximization and are currently experiencing the adaptability of a radical neoliberalism that is cementing its own existence with the diversification of the bourgeoisie and petty bourgeoisie. Liberal anti-racists promise us racism-sensitive capitalists, administrations and evening news, which are increasingly being presented by non-white Germans. However, those who seek to "shift the balance of power in the struggle against racist, gender-specific and other forms of oppression must not abstract from their material conditions and from the interest in maintaining them in order to stabilize relations of exploitation (Benhold et al, 2021: 30)."

However, this represents precisely the approach taken by liberal explanations of racism.

2 The Relation between Exploitation and Oppression

This volume represents an attempt to bring together Marxist-inspired explanations of racism in Germany and put them up for discussion. All the authors assembled here are united by the conviction that behind the economic class positions and the specific forms of exploitation associated with *race*, for example, lie different forms of social relations. In this context, class does not represent an identity or category of experience, but rather offers a structural explanation (Foley). In Marx, the class concept appears in various contexts:

> At times, as in the chapter on "The Working Day" in Volume I of Capital, it [class] is an empirical category, one inhabited by children who inhale factory dust, men who lose fingers in power-looms, women who drag barges, and slaves who pick cotton in the blazing sun [...] All these people are oppressed as well as exploited. But most of the time, for Marx, class is a relationship, a social relation of production; that is why, in the opening chapter of Capital, he can talk about the commodity, with its odd identity as a conjunction of use value and exchange value, as an embodiment of irreconcilable class antagonisms. To assert the priority of a class analysis is not to claim that a worker is more important than a homemaker, or even that the worker primarily thinks of herself as a worker; indeed, based on her personal experience with spousal abuse or police brutality, she may well think of herself more as a woman, or a black person. It is to propose, however, that the ways in which productive human activity is organized – and, in class-based society, compels the mass of the population to be divided up into various categories in order to insure that the many will be divided from one another and will labor for the benefit of the few – this class-based organization constitutes the principal issue requiring investigation if we wish to understand the roots of social inequality.
> Ibid

This programmatic approach emphasizes the centrality of the working class and the necessity of class-based organizing. It is not primarily about the specifically precarious life experiences of individuals, but about a horizon of human liberation for all. The concrete living conditions under the yoke of capital and the independent existence of ideological formations – such as racism, homo- and transhostility – are not irrelevant or unimportant. However, an understanding of society as something that has become opens up a perspective for everyone that makes it easier to understand exclusionary and violent experiences. An understanding of identity as a factor of capital relations opens up the possibility of placing ourselves in a different relation to ourselves, to class and to society. This allows me to situate my personal experience differently and thus relate differently to people who do not share my life experience, but who fight with me as a socialist against racism, homo- and transhostility.

Marxists today must analyze the situation in concrete terms and draw conclusions for corresponding politics. In our opinion, this includes a serious examination of the reasons for the current weakness of the left in Germany, what this failure has to do with its approach to racism, and how it relates to the successes and failures of the historical left.

It is our task not only to point out the shortcomings and flawed responses of others, but also to question ourselves in order to find a way out of new divisions and formations of new micro-groups. With regard to racism in Germany, there is a lack of analyses of the relation between contemporary racism and the history of German colonialism, and specifically whether other forms of colonial racism (especially in the Americas) have a stronger influence on, for example, the specific forms of anti-Black racism in Germany than German colonial history itself. Further analyses are required to determine the extent to which Germany's imperialist past has contributed to the current surge in racism, as well as to assess the impact of neoliberalism on racism. These and many other studies and discussions are still pending. With this volume, we hope to stimulate interest in Marxist theorizing and its further development, with a view to building on existing political debates and opening up the possibility for a revolutionary politics.

Bibliography

Benhold, Christin et al. (2021) Zur Kritik der Intersektionalität, *Z. Zeitschrift Marxistische Erneuerung*, vol. 126.

Breitman, George (1967) *Leon Trotsky on Black Nationalism & Self-Determination*. New York: Merit Publishers.

Foley, Barbara (2018) Intersectionality: A Marxist Critique, *Portside*, portside.org/2018-10-31/intersectionality-marxist-critique.

Lenin, Vladimir I. (1977) The Three Sources and Three Component Parts of Marxism, *Collected Works, Vol. 19*. Moscow: Progress Publishers.

Mariátegui, José Carlos (1974) The Problem of the Indian. In: José Carlos Mariátegui, *Seven Interpretative Essays on Peruvian Reality*. Austin: University of Texas Press.

Reed Jr, Adolph (2013) Marx, Race and Neoliberalism, *New Labor Forum*, vol. 22, no. 1, pp. 49–57, DOI: 10.1177/1095796012471637.

Rodney, Walter (1975) Marxism and African Liberation, marxists.org/subject/africa/rodney-walter/works/marxismandafrica.htm.

Index

Africa, African, Africans 6, 8, 18–20, 23–24, 43–44, 56, 86, 135
ally, allyship 3
anti-colonial 17, 20, 42, 44, 132
anti-racist 3, 68
Asia, Asian x, 7, 25

Bhattacharya, Tithi 38, 54
Black feminsm 70
black radical tradition 6, 8
border, borders 42, 51, 57, 59–62, 84, 100, 115, 132–133

citizenship 46–47, 61, 96, 98, 100, 102, 125, 127
colonial, colonialism xvi, 6–9, 11, 17–21, 23–24, 29–31, 41–44, 54, 80, 85–87, 138
criminalization 83, 85, 87, 91
crisis xi, 26–27, 31, 36, 47, 102, 114, 117–123, 125, 127, 133

discrimination, anti vii–viii, x, 3, 16, 28–29, 45–46, 58, 61–62, 66–67, 70–71, 73–74, 76
decolonial, decoloniality xvi
domination vii, 1, 6, 9, 21, 32, 51–57, 59–62, 91, 132–133

Engels, Frederick 2, 4–7, 39, 135, 136
ethnicity 11
eurocentric, eurocentrism 7, 8
European Union (EU) 59–61, 96–104, 107–108, 122, 134

Farris, Sara 46, 133
feminism xv, xviii, 38, 42, 44, 66, 69, 70, 74, 127
femonationalism 46, 133
Fraser, Nancy 58, 127

gender vii, ix, 6, 10, 17, 36–48, 54, 55, 66, 67, 70, 73, 74, 76, 77, 115, 118, 119, 124, 125, 132, 133, 136
guest workers 25–28, 44, 45

Hanau xvii, 89
hegemony 38, 117, 118

identity politics viii, ix, xv, xviii, 3, 69, 70, 73, 127
ideology 2, 4, 8, 17, 21, 23, 24, 30, 32, 33, 47, 52, 116–118, 121, 125, 126, 133
intersectionality viii, xii, xvii, 66, 69–77, 133, 134

James, C.L.R. 135

Latin America xi, 8, 37, 43
Lenin, Vladimir Illich 1, 2, 135
liberalism 2, 33

manichaeism 23
Mariátegui, José Carlos 135
Marx, Karl x, 1, 2, 4–8, 17–20, 25, 33, 39, 53, 54, 71, 72, 77, 80, 81, 83, 85, 89, 91, 135–137
materialism/materialist 1, 4, 11, 17, 33, 37, 38, 41, 53, 54, 56, 57, 58, 62, 114, 117
materialism/materialism, dialectical 2, 8, 12, 37, 67
materialism/materialist, historical 12, 17, 29, 31, 37, 40, 52, 62
metropole 19, 20–23
migration 24–27, 33, 45–47, 51, 52, 54, 57–62, 73, 74, 80, 81, 90, 95–97, 100–102, 104–108, 119, 132–134

National Socialism 26
Neoliberal, neoliberalism ix, 29, 44, 46, 58, 59, 62, 70, 88, 115, 116, 119, 120, 121, 122, 123, 125, 126, 134, 136
neo-racism 24, 48

oppression vii, viii, 10, 20, 32, 37, 38, 40, 41, 44, 66–74, 76, 77
original accumulation 18, 19, 54, 72

pre-colonial 18
production vii, x, xvi, xviii, 2, 6, 7, 10, 17–21, 24, 25, 30, 32, 36–41, 43, 45, 47, 51–56, 59, 61, 62, 71, 72, 74, 76, 80–83, 86, 89, 95, 96, 99, 103–108, 117, 132, 133, 135, 136
progressive-neoliberal 59, 62
policing 81, 88, 90
postcolonialism, postcolonial theory xvi, 7, 75

queer   41, 115, 118

racial capitalism   XVI, 8–10, 13
racialization   XVI, 17, 23, 25, 28, 30, 43, 47
reification   X, 42, 70, 71, 76, 134
Robinson, Cedric   7–10
Rodney, Walter   8, 17, 20, 22, 87, 135

slaves   18, 83, 137
slavery   XVI, 5, 6, 16, 18–20, 44, 56, 86
socialist   XV, 3–5, 8, 39, 48, 67, 68, 70, 74–77, 126, 127, 136, 137
super-exploitation   10, 12, 20–23, 25, 26, 29, 30, 32, 39, 42, 43, 54, 62, 68, 71, 81, 86, 89, 91, 95, 96, 104, 132–134

totality   2, 23, 33, 52, 56
trade union, trade unions   IX, X, 26, 45, 57, 62, 68, 106, 107, 108, 109
triple oppression   XII, 69

underdeveloped   22, 30
universalism   8, 75

Vogel, Lise   38, 40

wage labor   6, 19–21, 36, 38, 39 54, 56, 82–85, 87, 90, 100, 101, 123
world system   52

xenophobia   16, 29

www.ingramcontent.com/pod-product-compliance
Lightning Source LLC
Chambersburg PA
CBHW070629030426
42337CB00020B/3962